MW00465190

# EXTREME RETIREMENT SOLUTIONS

**EX·TREME - IK'STRĒM/** ADJECTIVE: REACHING A
HIGH OR THE HIGHEST DEGREE; VERY GREAT.

## DAVID R. NAGY, IAR

Printed in the United States of America

First Printing, 2017

Gradient Positioning Systems, LLC
4105 Lexington Avenue North, Suite 110
Arden Hills, MN 55126
(877) 901-0894

Contributors: Nick Stovall, Mike Binger, Nate Lucius and Gradient Positioning Systems, LLC.

# TABLE OF CONTENTS

# DEDICATION

I dedicate this book to my mom and dad, Elaine and Robert Nagy. I wouldn't be the man I am today without their love, support and guidance. Thank you, mom, for the example of your caring and compassionate energy. Thank you, dad, for teaching me how to use my hands and solve problems with confidence and ingenuity. Your values of courage, family and living life to its fullest are the models I aspire to every single day. Thank you for giving me the road map to such a wonderful life.

# INTRODUCTION

*"Live life while there's life to live because this isn't a dress rehearsal."*
– Elaine Nagy

*I've always been a thrill seeker. My father gave me the adventure bug at a young age, and I grew up waterskiing and sailing, playing ice hockey and surfing the biggest waves I could find. It was while paddling out one day through the waves that I realized I was having a hard time breathing. I thought, at the age of 24, I've never had a physical and I'd better get that checked out. I made an appointment and when the x-rays came back, the doctor was shocked. "There's something in your lung," he said, and ordered a CAT scan. I wasn't too alarmed. I was young, healthy and active. I thought, how bad can it really be? Then I met the radiologist and did he scare the crap out of me. "David," he said, in a very serious tone, "You have a large mass in your lung about the size of a small cantaloupe."*

1

*I sat down, speechless. My doctor hadn't used the word, mass. He just said something was there. That afternoon, I entered into an entirely different reality.*

*The radiologist showed me the images from my CAT scan. The left lung was clean, while in the right lung, there was the giant white spot of a tumor. There were also spots in my abdomen and tumors the size of golf balls in my neck, pushing my esophagus closed. We scheduled another appointment with my doctor and I was referred to a great oncologist.*

*Dr. Joan Kroner set up a time to meet with my entire family and me. First, she called me alone into an exam room, explained the situation, what the treatment would be and said since I was young and in great shape the outlook was promising. Dr. Kroner asked me if I had any questions and the first thing that came to my mind was "when do we get started?" In my mind it never occurred to me that I could or would die. The sooner I could start treatment the sooner I could go on with my life! Now it was time to break the news to my family. When Dr. Kroner called us into the room to announce my diagnosis, Hodgkin's Lymphoma, I looked over and saw my mom crying. I did not like seeing my mother crying and wanting to reassure her everything would be okay. I looked at her and said, "Mom, don't worry I'm going to be okay." What she said next surprised me. "Oh David," she said, "I'm not crying because I'm worried, I'm crying because we're happy! We knew you had cancer, but we didn't know what kind. Hodgkin's at your age is very curable!" I had no Idea that my family already knew I had cancer and they had been researching all the different possibilities and treatments. They were praying for a diagnosis of Hodgkin's!*

*And so I started my fight.*

*At the time I was living in San Diego, employed as foreman at a thriving construction outfit based in California. I couldn't continue that kind of physical labor along with my chemotherapy, so I entered into a time of unemployment/disability. My job was battling*

*Hodgkin's. I would go for my treatment in the morning, and they would sedate me heavily because this was before they had approved the anti-nausea drugs used today. I would pass out during the chemo, someone would drive me home, and then I would throw up for the next 24 hours. The first few days felt like you had really bad food poisoning, then it tapered off to a kind of flu. By the end of the 7th day, you felt almost normal, like recovering from a bad cold. You got one week after that of feeling somewhat normal. I would go to the beach, look at the waves, try to surf. Then I would start the process all over again. I did that for six months.*

*Following chemo, I went through nine and a half weeks of daily radiation. They burned my skin off from my chin down to my belly button. It turned black and peeled away. Because the radiation was daily, it felt even worse than the chemo. I had no saliva, eating had become almost painful and I had to throw corn starch under my arms to avoid chafing.*

*Then came the day my oncologist put up the CAT scans again and we took a look. Everything was clear, except for a small bit of scar tissue on my right lung. "We'll need to watch that," she said. "If the cancer comes back, that's where it would start." I set up an appointment for three months' time and waited. The next x-ray revealed that the scar tissue had gotten bigger. This was the first time during the whole ordeal I was really afraid.*

*During all those months of fighting, I never really believed I would die until that moment. For the first time it occurred to me that I might die. The reality of it hit me, and a voice in my head said, "Hey, life is precious. You'd better make the most of the time you are given." That moment of realization has always stayed with me even now, over 26 years later, because I did get a second chance. Dr. Kroner explained to me that sometimes, radiation affects scar tissue and that it later shrinks back down. We waited another three months and took another CAT scan. I'll never forget that October, attending a Halloween event at my local church with my girlfriend. I remember that evening with particular clarity, the families who were walking around, all the happy kids, because I was waiting to find out if I would live or die. Then by chance my oncologist turned up at the event. She came over to me and said, "David, I have really great news for you. The scar tissue shrank back down and you are officially in remission."*

*I started crying right there, because I knew I was given a second chance at life and I was going to live.*

While I would never choose to go through what I went through, my battle with cancer and the subsequent years working as a counselor and spokesperson for the American Cancer Society taught me something very valuable. I saw at a very young age how really, we are all the same. All of us have expectations, desires and fears. We only have so much time here on earth to fulfill those desires. This realization has made me a better person and a better financial professional, because I understand that what you do with your fears in large part determines the success of your living.

Retirement is a time of major change set against the backdrop of a great deal of fear. Will taxes go up? Will the dollar fall? Will the actions of terrorist groups crash our economy? The stock market is volatile, interest rates are low and the national debt is rising higher. How do you plan for a secure retirement in the face of so much uncertainty?

The fear can be immobilizing, which is why I am so passionate about what I do. This book is here to guide you through a process of asset allocation that shows you why you don't need to expose yourself to risk in order to have a successful retirement. With proper planning and strategizing, you can create an income for life that you'll never outlive, no matter how long you live. As a financial professional in the business of helping people secure income, I want you to understand your choices and options so you can be in control. After a lifetime of working hard and saving, you deserve to be happy. You deserve the opportunity to create a life you love living. On the day you retire, that's when a whole new adventure becomes available to you.

## SECRETS OF THE NEWLY UNEMPLOYED

My dad was pretty upset when I took up skydiving. After surviving cancer, however, I lived for a period of ten years under the shadow that it might come back. So I started living hard and working hard. I decided to change professions and studied for and passed my securities and insurance license tests. I decided to make a skydive with a friend. From my first jump I realized there was something about skydiving you just can't get from any other activity. When you jump out of an aircraft from 12,500 feet, something changes. You feel alive, you aren't thinking about your bills, relationships, or work. Nothing else matters. You are 100 percent in the moment. It's an amazing feeling that I think everyone should experience at least once in their lifetime.

I became so addicted to the sport that I started filming sky diving videos; I became a Tandem instructor; and I became a certified AFF (accelerated free-fall) instructor. I traveled all around the world scuba diving, skydiving and surfing. I scuba dove in, Belize, Cozumel, Guam and Hawaii; raced cars in Baja; and surfed waves all the way from Costa Rica to South Africa. My dad kept asking me, "Why do you have a death wish, son?" And I explained to him about risk and safety. I never felt like I was going to die when skydiving because I'm extremely safety conscious. I practice my emergency procedures, go through all the possible scenarios, and prepare for every possible situation.

This is the same thing I do when helping people prepare for retirement. When you understand the risks, you can prepare for them. By having your retirement income set up in vehicles that are safe and secure (your parachute), you can afford more risk with your other assets.

Whether we are suiting up for a jump or getting our gear together for a dive, the one thing that can kill you is running out of air. With ocean diving, this air is dependent on your oxygen tank; with sky diving, it's the air beneath you that you don't want to run out before your chute opens. This can be compared to running out of money during retirement. If you prepare for the risks ahead of time, before you jump out of the plane—or stop working—then you can enjoy the ride knowing the parachute of your lifetime income will deploy. Which brings up the question: Who is packing your parachute? Are you doing it alone, or with the help of a financial professional? If you do have help, how certain are you that your professional has your back covered?

Skydivers never jump out of an airplane with only one parachute. They always have a back-up chute. Scuba divers also check and recheck their gear and bring backup oxygen in case something goes wrong.

Here you are, getting ready to retire, and you look around at all the gear you have accumulated for the adventure. This gear can be compared to your investments, your assets, the 401(k) savings plans or IRAs. You have been focused up to this point on getting all this gear together, which means you've been focused on the rate of return. But here's the thing: We are about to enter into a whole new phase of life. You are about to jump out of the retirement plane, which means you need the gear to go to work for you. You want that parachute to open! The best rate of return in the world isn't going to help you if that chute doesn't deploy and you can't pay the bills. This highlights the biggest difference between your working years and your retired years:

*During retirement, you are unemployed for life.* That means it's time for your assets to go to work for you. When you think about your assets in terms of the income they can produce, and realize that retirement is a period of 20 or more years, you start to see why your focus needs to shift off the rate of return and onto the ability of an investment to provide you with what you really need: a safe and reliable paycheck for life.

## THE THREE MAJOR CHANGES COMING YOUR WAY

Perhaps the worst mistake you can make as a retiree is to do nothing and keep your assets positioned in their current vehicles designed for accumulation and growth. It is difficult to know where to move your money in today's economy, but education and understanding can serve as antidotes to this fear. As a person entering into retirement and joining the ranks of the newly unemployed, you'll notice three major changes taking place that influence the amount of income you'll need and the kinds of investments and strategies you'll want to consider.

1. **Changes to your lifestyle**: You are used to working a 40 to 60-hour workweek, then coming home and fitting in all the other things you want to do. When you retire, you'll find yourself with all this free time. Finally, you'll have the time to do more of the things you want to do. While many experts purport that during retirement, people scale back, today's Baby Boomers are retiring strong with a lot more life left in them. In 1950, the average man lived to the age of 65. Today, most men can expect to live until the age of 86 and women are likely to live even longer.* That means the average 65-year-old retiree today needs to plan for more than 20 years of income. The Financial Overview and The Rule of 100 Report covered in Chapter 1 will help you prepare your assets to accommodate your lifestyle needs so your money can last as long as you do.

2. **Changes to your risk tolerance**: When you retire, your attitude about risk should change. During your working

---

* *http://www.ncbi.nlm.nih.gov/books/NBK62373/*

years, how did you feel about losing money when the market was down? You weren't likely happy about it, but you knew you had time to make up for the loss, and you were still putting money into those investments. During retirement, however, no more money is going into those investments. Now, you are taking money out. As an aspiring retiree or newly retired person, how do you feel about losing money now that you have no more earned income? Chapter 2 takes a look at the risks your assets are exposed to using the Color of Money concept. Chapter 3 goes over the basics of creating an income plan and your first legacy: what you leave behind for your spouse.

3. **Changes to your savings:** Most people retiring today can expect to receive some income in the form of their Social Security benefit. Chapter 4 explains filing options and strategies and why you want to look at this benefit in terms of a *lifetime income source.* What other sources of guaranteed income do you have? Your savings likely represent one source of guaranteed income you will rely on during retirement. Some people use their savings a little; others will need to use them a lot. Knowing how to withdraw money from your savings in a way that is sustainable for the long term is the focus of the rest of this book. Chapter 5 takes you through an education about today's new income creation vehicles and the benefits they can provide for those seeking alternative solutions to long-term care. Chapters 6 and 8 explain the difference between accumulation and growth strategies used during your working years as compared to retirement. Chapters 9 through 11 address taxes, and Chapters 12 and 13 talk about preparing your legacy. Estate planning is an area often overlooked by a lot of financial planners. Proper planning means we are committed to making sure that

you are taken care of, not just with regard to the financial aspect, but in every aspect of retirement.

## SUCCESSFUL RETIREMENT SOLUTIONS

Serving southern California, Arizona and Nevada, and with over 26 years of experience in the financial industry, Successful Retirement Solutions, LLC. is about creating income and peace of mind. The mission of our firm is to ensure your idea of a happy retirement through the use of creative financial solutions backed by unparalleled personal service.

My own personal philosophy is to live life like you might die tomorrow, while planning like you might live forever. I understand better than most what kinds of risks you are taking when fear has you stuck. There's no reason why you have to spend retirement lying in bed at night, awake and worried about your future. Let me show you how to design a plan that will give you the freedom to enjoy the ride and live the life waiting for you.

– David R. Nagy

Investment advisor representative and owner of Successful Retirement Solutions, LLC.

# 1

# THE VIEW FROM ABOVE

*"I suspected skydiving was dangerous when they asked me
to sign a waiver. They confirmed my suspicions when
they asked me to pay in advance."*
– Author Unknown

*Will your Social Security benefit, savings and other retirement assets
be enough? If you're like Buzz and Tamara, you hope so. When the
couple turned 60 years old, they started thinking about what their
lives would be like in the next 10 years. When would they retire?
What would their retirement look like? How much money did they
have?*

*Tamara had a 401(k) plan through her employer, but she wasn't
exactly sure how it worked, how she could draw money from it and
how much income it would provide once she retired. Buzz had some
investments he'd made over the years and a small pension he would*

*receive, but the pension wasn't nearly enough to support their income needs. They were also both entitled to Social Security, but neither one really knew how much their monthly checks would be, or when to file for them. Tamara signed up for a retirement planning seminar to learn more about their options, but Buzz grumbled and didn't want to go. So Tamara went by herself. Afterwards, she was so convinced that if they didn't sit down and do some proper planning now, all their hard work and years of saving would be in jeopardy. She made an appointment with the financial professional and this time, Buzz came along.*

*During the first meeting, Buzz was surprised to find that he did most of the talking. He had a lot on his mind, and the financial professional took notes and listened. He then ran a series of reports for them that revealed what Tamara had suspected—if the stock market made a correction tomorrow, they would lose a large portion of the money they needed to rely on for their retirement income. The problem was clear: they had their assets set up for growth and accumulation. Their financial professional also showed them several strategies and solutions that would solve the problem and bring them the income they would need.*

*When it was time to go, Buzz thanked the financial professional all the way to the door. "This was exactly what I needed to do," he said, "I can't tell you how much better I feel."*

While Buzz and Tamara may sound like they're totally in the dark about their retirement, the truth is there are a lot of people just like them. They know retirement is coming and know they have some assets to rely on, but they aren't sure how it will all come together to provide them with a retirement income.

You spend your entire working life hoping what you put into your retirement accounts will help you live comfortably once you clock out of the workforce for good. The key word in that sentiment and the word that can make retirement feel like a looming problem instead of a rewarding life stage, is *hope*. You hope you'll have enough money.

Leaving your retirement up to chance is unadvisable by nearly any standard, yet millions of people find themselves *hoping* instead of planning for a happy ending. With information, tools and professional guidance, creating a successful retirement plan can put you in control of your financial management.

While you may have built up a 401(k), an IRA, and Social Security benefits, do you know what your financial picture really looks like?

Structuring assets to create an income-generating retirement requires a different approach than earning income via the workforce. Saving money for retirement, which is what you have spent your life doing, and *planning* your retirement are two different things. During retirement, it is the job of the savings you have worked so hard to build up to provide you with the means to maintain the lifestyle you are accustomed to. What you choose to do with your savings now (in the years just prior to and during retirement) in large part determines the success of your retirement.

Money represents more than the paper it's printed on. It is the embodiment of your time, your talents, and your commitments. It buys the food you eat, the house you sleep in, the car you drive, and the clothes you wear. It also helps provide you with the lifestyle you want to live once you retire.

You have spent a lifetime earning it, spending it, and hopefully, accumulating it. When the time comes for retirement, you want your money to provide you with a comfortable lifestyle and stable income after your working days are done. You might also have other desires, such as traveling, purchasing property, or moving to be closer to your family (or farther away). You may also want your assets to provide for your loved ones after you are gone.

The truth is that it takes more than just money to fulfill those needs and desires. Your income, your plans for retirement, your future healthcare expenses, and the continued accumulation of your assets after you stop working and drawing a paycheck all rely on one thing: *You.*

Think of it like this: You took time to choose your career, your educational path, your employment experience, and the time and talent required to develop your professional skill-set. You chose a profession or a line of work that matched your skills and talents with your income needs and lifestyle choices. You did this to suit your needs and preferences, to give you the salary you desired, and to do the work you were interested in and good at performing.

Creating a retirement plan requires the same crafting and care that you put into your career. Your assets, your income needs, and your lifestyle are different than your neighbor's, and you need a retirement plan that reflects your needs, not theirs or anyone else's.

It is a truism among financial professionals that ***one hour of organizing your assets can be worth more than an entire lifetime of working and saving*** when it comes to retirement.

## YOUR FINANCIAL OVERVIEW REPORT

From a purely financial perspective, the primary challenge of planning for a long, secure retirement is preparing for the day your paycheck stops and you need to turn a lifetime of savings into an income you cannot outlive. It is something quite unlike any financial challenge you have faced before.

Solving this challenge is about more than just choosing from among a handful of investments. Not only are there thousands of different options for each individual that affect when and how to file for Social Security benefits, there are a multitude of different strategies for how to structure your other assets like individual retirement accounts (IRAs), 401(k)s, life insurance policies, and investment portfolios. Choosing the best solutions for your individual situation must begin with an examination of where you are currently at. Your financial professional will need to get to know the lay of the land, so to speak, before he or she can make any recommendations. Before the individual investments are examined, however, the individuals themselves must be understood.

- What does retirement look like for you?
- What are your goals?
- What are your fears?
- Who are the people you want to take care of?
- What are some of the things you want to do during retirement?

Once we have identified your goals, the next step is to take a look at your current asset allocation. There are over 25 different reports or tests a financial professional can run for you. These reports help assess the performance of your current investments in order to determine whether or not they support your retirement goals. These reports give you a bird's eye view, so to speak, of your current situation. Your financial professional will choose which reports to run for you based on what you say your goals are. For example, consider Craig and Kristen:

» *Craig and Kristen have been contributing to their IRAs for the last 25 years, but they don't want to use the money for their income needs. It is their goal to leave this money for their kids. Upon learning of this goal, their financial professional runs several reports. The first is The Financial Overview Report, and it shows them that Craig and Kristen do have enough assets in their respective 401(k)s to structure for their income needs if they reallocate the funds based on other the report recommendations. Once the money needed for their income is reallocated into secure income producing vehicles, their financial professional runs a Legacy Report. This report shows them how best to set up their IRAs in order to leave the maximum amount to their kids and grandkids.* ***Craig and Kristen*** *had no idea that there were different ways to set up an IRA. The report calculates how they can leave their children 42 percent more money simply by avoiding taxes and structuring their IRAs properly for beneficiary distribution.*

**The Financial Overview Report** is one report that everyone can benefit from when starting their income plan. It gives you the view from above by showing you exactly where you are at right now. It lists all the assets in each of your accounts, starting with the amounts you have in your bank accounts, savings, investment and brokerage accounts. It also lists any outstanding loans, real estate property and residence property.

The report then delves into potential sources for income. It takes a look at Social Security benefit and pension amounts. It also shows potential sources for income in risk accounts such as stocks, mutual funds, REITs and ETFs. Then going further, it looks at the assets in safe money accounts such as bank CDs, bonds and money market accounts. The Financial Overview Reports is like a snapshot in time of where you stand now. Once we identify a starting point, we can then look at how best to position these assets so they can support you for the long ride ahead.

*Making sure your assets last for your lifetime will depend on how you decide to invest them, and in what order you will spend them.*

With forces like inflation, market volatility, and fluctuating interest rates working against you, knowing what to do with your assets has never been more important. And the difference between making a good decisions and a bad decision has never had such a dramatic impact on how people retire.

*The question isn't CAN you or SHOULD you put your money to work for you and your family. It's HOW.*

## NEW IDEAS FOR RETIREMENT

Advice about what to do with money has been around as long as money has existed. Hindsight allows us to see which advice was good and which advice didn't cut the mustard. Some sources of advice have been around for a very long time. While there are some basic investment concepts that have stood the test of time, most strategies that work adapt to changing conditions in the market, in the economy and the world, as well as changes in your personal circumstances.

The reality is that investment strategies and savings plans that worked in the past have encountered challenging new circumstances that have turned them on their heads. The Great Recession of the early 2000's highlighted how old investment ideas were not only ineffective but incredibly destructive to the retirement plans of millions of Americans. The dawn of an entirely restructured health care system brings with it new options and challenges that will undoubtedly change the way insurance companies provide investment products and services.

Perhaps the most important lessons investors learned from the Great Recession is that not understanding where your money is invested (and the potential risks of those investments) can work against you, your plans for retirement and your legacy. Saving and investing money isn't enough to truly get the most out of it. You must have a planful approach to managing your assets.

Essentially, managing your money and your investments is an ongoing process that requires customization and adaptation to a changing world. And make no mistake; the world is always changing. What worked for your parents or even your parents' parents was probably good advice back then. People in retirement or approaching retirement today need new ideas and professional guidance.

## HOPE SO VS. KNOW SO MONEY

Let's take a look at some of the basic truths about money as it relates to saving for retirement.

There are essentially two kinds of money: *Hope So* and *Know So.* Everyone can divide their money into these two categories. Some have more of one kind than the other. The goal isn't to eliminate one kind of money but to balance them as you approach retirement.

**Hope So Money** is money that is at risk.
- It fluctuates with the market.
- It has no minimum guarantee.
- It is subject to investor activity, stock prices, market trends, buying trends, etc.

You get the picture. This money is exposed to more risk but also has the potential for more reward. Because the market is subject to change, you can't really be sure what the value of your investments will be worth in the future. You can't really *rely* on it at all. For this reason, we refer to it as Hope So Money. This doesn't mean you shouldn't have some money invested in the market, but it would be dangerous to assume you can know what it will be worth in the future.

Hope So Money is an important element of a retirement plan, especially in the early stages of planning when you can trade volatility for potential returns, and when a longer investment timeframe is available to you. In the long run, time can smooth out the ups and downs of money exposed to the market. Working with a professional and leveraging a long-term investment strategy has the potential to create rewarding returns from Hope So Money.

**Know So Money**, on the other hand, is safer when compared to Hope So Money.
- It is dependable.
- It is low-risk or no-risk.
- It is made up of investments that you can count on.

Social Security is one of the most common forms of Know So Money. Income you draw or will draw from Social Security is guaranteed. You have paid into Social Security your entire career, and you can rely on that money during your retirement. Unlike the market, rates of growth for Know So Money are dependent on 10-year treasury rates. The 10-year treasury, or TNX, is com-

Source – Yahoo Finance – 11-31-2018
VIX is a trademarked ticker symbol for the Chicago Board Options Exchange Market Volatility index, a popular measure of the implied volatility of S&P 500 index options. Often referred to as the fear index or the fear gauge, it represents one measure of the market's expectation of stock market volatility over the next 30 day period. (www.investopedia.com/terms/v/vix.asp) The CBOE 10-Year Treasury Note (TNX) is based on 10 times the yield-to-maturity on the most recently auctioned 10 year Treasury note. This chart is for illustrative purposes and not intended to be representative of any specific investment vehicle. Past performance does not guarantee future results. Some illustrations may show how a market index has performed. An investor cannot invest in an index, although there are some investments designed to mirror index performance. Past performance is not a guarantee of future results.

*The VIX, or volatility index, of the market represents expected market volatility. When the VIX Drops, economic experts expect less volatility. When the VIX rises, more volatility is expected.*

1. *VIX is a trademarked ticker symbol for the Chicago Board Options Exchange (CBOE) Market Volatility Index, a popular measure of the implied volatility of S&P 500 index options. Often referred to as the fear index or the fear gauge, it represents one measure of the market's expectation of stock market volatility over the next 30 day period. (wikipedia.com)*

2. *The CBOE 10-Year Treasury note (TNX) is based on 10 times the yield-to-maturity on the most recently auctioned 10-year Treasury note.*

monly considered to represent a very secure and safe place for your money, hence Know So Money. The 10-year treasury drives key rates for things such as mortgage rates or CD rates. Know So Money may not be as exciting as Hope So Money, but it is safer. You can safely be fairly sure you will have it in the future.

Knowing the difference between Hope So and Know So Money is an important step towards a successful retirement plan. People who are 55 or older and who are looking ahead to retirement should be relying on more Know So Money than Hope So Money.

Ideally, the rates of return on Hope So and Know So Money would have an overlapping area that provided an acceptable rate of risk for both types of money. In the early 1990s, interest rates were high and market volatility was low. At that time, you could invest in either Hope So or Know So Money options because the rates of return were similar from both Know So and Hope So investments, and you were likely to be fairly successful with a wide range of investment options. At that time, you could expose yourself to an acceptable amount of risk or an acceptable fixed rate. Basically, it was difficult to make a mistake during that time period. Today, you don't have those options. Market volatility is at all-time highs while interest rates are at all-time lows. They are so far apart from each other that it is hard to know what to do with your money.

Yesterday's investment rules may not work today. Not only could they hamper achieving your goals, they may actually harm your financial situation. We are currently in a period when the rates for Know So Money options are at historic lows, and the volatility of Hope So Money is higher than ever. There is no overlapping acceptable rate, making both options less than ideal. *Because of this uncertain financial landscape, wise investment strategies are more important now than ever.*

This unique situation requires fresh ideas and investment tools that haven't been relied on in the past. Investing the way your parents did will not pay off. The majority of investment ideas used by financial professionals in the 1990s aren't applicable to today's markets. That kind of investing will likely get you in trouble and compromise your retirement. Today, you need a better PLAN.

## HOW MUCH RISK ARE YOU EXPOSED TO?

Many investors don't know how much risk they are exposed to. It is helpful to organize your assets so you can have a clear understanding of how much of your money is at risk and how much is in safer holdings. This process starts with listing all your assets.

Let's take a look again at the two kinds of money:

**Hope So Money** is, as the name indicates, money that you *hope* will be there when you need it. Hope So Money represents what you would like to get out of your investments. Examples of Hope So Money include:
- Stock market funds, including index funds
- Mutual funds
- Variable annuities
- REITS

**Know So Money** is money that you know you can count on. It is safer money that isn't exposed to the level of volatility as the asset types noted above. You can more confidently count on having this money when you need it. Examples of Know So Money are:
- Government backed bonds
- Savings and checking accounts
- Fixed income annuities
- CDs
- Treasuries
- Money market accounts

» *Michael had a modest brokerage account that he added to when he could. When he changed jobs a couple years ago, at age 58, Michael transferred his 401(k) assets into an IRA. Just a few years from retirement, he is now beginning to realize that nearly every dollar he has saved for retirement is subject to market risk.*

*Intuitively, he knows that the time has come to shift some assets to an alternative that is safer, but how much is the right amount?*

## THE RULE OF 100 REPORT

The average investor needs to accumulate assets to create a retirement plan that provides income during retirement and also allows for legacy planning. To accomplish this, they need to balance the amount of risk to which they are exposed. Risk is required because, while Know So Money is safer, more reliable and more dependable, it doesn't grow very fast, if at all. Today's historically low interest rates barely break even with current inflation. Hope So Money, while less dependable, has more potential for growth. Hope So Money can eventually become Know So Money once you move it to an investment with lower risk. Everyone's risk diversification will be different depending on their goals, age and their existing assets.

So how do you decide how much risk your assets should be exposed to? Where do you begin?

While there is no single approach to investment risk determination advice that is universally applicable to everyone, there are some helpful guidelines. One of the most useful is called *The Rule of 100.* The Rule of 100 is a general rule that helps shape asset diversification* for the average investor. The rule states that the number 100 minus an investor's age equals the amount of assets they should have exposed to risk.

**The Rule of 100**: 100 - (your age) = the percentage of your assets that should be exposed to risk (Hope So Money).

For example, if you are a 30-year-old investor, the Rule of 100 would indicate that you should be focusing on investing primarily in the market and taking on a substantial amount of risk in your portfolio. The Rule of 100 suggests that 70 percent of your investments should be exposed to risk.

$$100 - (30 \text{ years of age}) = 70 \text{ percent}$$

Now, not every 30-year-old should have exactly 70 percent of their assets in mutual funds and stocks. The Rule of 100 Report is based on your chronological age, not your "financial age," which could vary based on your investment experience, your aversion or acceptance of risk and other factors. While this rule isn't an ironclad solution to anyone's finances, it's a pretty good place to

* *Asset Diversification disclosure – Diversification and asset allocation does not assure or guarantee better performance and cannot eliminate the risk of investment loss. Before investing, you should carefully read the applicable volatility disclosure for each of the underlying funds, which can be found in the current prospectus.*

start. Once you've taken the time to look at your assets with a professional to determine your risk exposure, you can use the Rule of 100 to make changes that put you in a more stable investment position—one that reflects your comfort level.

First and foremost, the Rule of 100 Report gives you a picture of your current portfolio as compared to your suggested portfolio. On one page, it shows your current asset allocations using a pie chart so you can visualize the percentage of Know So Money investments, compared to Hope So Money investments. On the next page, it shows a suggested amount of assets to move in order to achieve a balanced portfolio for your individual situation. A lot of people are surprised by how much Hope So Money their portfolio has. This largely has to do with where you have been— your accumulation years. The investments used to help grow your portfolio when you were employed are not necessarily the best investments for you to rely on during your unemployed time during retirement.

## WHERE YOU HAVE BEEN AND WHERE YOU ARE GOING

Perhaps when you were age 30 and starting your career, it made sense to have 70 percent of your money in the market: you had time on your side. You had plenty of time to save more money, work more and recover from a downturn in the market. Retirement was ages away, and your earning power was increasing. And indeed, younger investors should take on more risk for exactly those reasons. The potential reward of long-term involvement in the market outweighs the risk of investing when you are young.

**Risk tolerance generally reduces as you get older, however.** If you are 40 years old and lose 30 percent of your portfolio in a market downturn this year, you have 20 or 30 years to recover it. If you are 68 years old, you have five to 10 years (or less) to make the same recovery. That new circumstance changes your whole retirement perspective. At age 68, it's likely that you simply aren't as interested in suffering through a tough stock market. There is less time to recover from downturns, and the stakes are higher. The money you have saved is money you will soon need to provide you with income, or is money that you already need to meet your income demands.

Much of the flexibility that comes with investing earlier in life is related to *compounding*. Compounded earnings can be incredibly powerful over time. The longer your money has time to compound, the greater your wealth will be. This is what most people talk about when they refer to putting their money to work. This is also why the Rule of 100 favors risk for the young. If you start investing when you are young, you can invest smaller amounts of money in a more aggressive fashion because you have the potential to make a profit in a rising market and you can harness the power of compounding earnings. When you are 40, 50 or 60 years old, that potential becomes less and less and you are forced to have more money at lower amounts of risk to realize the same returns. **It basically becomes more expensive to prudently invest the older you get.**

You risk not having a recovery period the older you get, so should have less of your assets at risk in volatile investments. You should shift with the Rule of 100 to protect your assets and ensure that they will provide you with the income you need in retirement. Let's look at another example that illustrates how the Rule of 100 becomes more critical as you age. An 80-year-old investor who is retired and is relying on retirement assets for income, for example, needs to depend on a solid amount of Know So Money. The Rule of 100 says an 80-year-old investor should have a maximum of 20 percent of his or her assets at risk. Depending on the investor's financial position, even less risk exposure may be required. You are the only person who can make this kind of determination, but the Rule of 100 can help. Everyone has their own level of comfort.

Your Rule of 100 results will be based on your values and attitudes as well as your comfort with risk.

The Rule of 100 can apply to overarching financial management and to specific investment products that you own as well. Take the 401(k) for example. Many people have them, but not many people understand how their money is allocated within their 401(k). An employer may have someone who comes in once a year and explains the models and options that employees can choose from, but that's as much guidance as most 401(k) holders get. Many 401(k) options include target date funds that change their risk exposure over time, essentially following a form of the Rule of 100. Selecting one of these options can often be a good move for employees because they shift your risk as you age, securing more Know So Money when you need it.

So, what does the Rule of 100 mean to you? Determining the amount of risk that is right for you is dependent on a number of variables. You need to feel comfortable with where and how you are investing your money, and your financial professional is obligated to help you make decisions that put your money in places that fit your risk criteria. A financial professional can look at your assets with you as part of your financial overview and discuss alternatives to optimize your balance between Know So and Hope So Money. Furthermore, there are other helpful reports that he or she can run that will do more to reveal which solutions will lead you towards the most successful retirement.

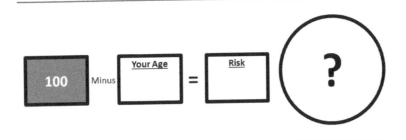

## CHAPTER 1 RECAP //

- There is money you hope you'll have in the future, and there's money you know you'll have in the future. Make sure you know how much you need when you retire.
- Organizing your assets starts with understanding your goals and taking a look at how you are currently positioned. The Financial Overview Report gives you a bird's eye view of all your assets. You can then utilize the help of other reports to understand how each asset is balanced for risk.
- Your exposure to risk is ultimately determined by you.
- Use the Rule of 100 as a general guiding principle when determining how much risk your retirement investments should be exposed to (100 - [your age] = [percentage of your investments that can comfortably exposed to risk]).

# 2

# UNDERSTANDING RISK:
## WHY SLOW IS SMOOTH AND SMOOTH IS FAST

*"The one thing that unites all human beings, regardless of age, gender, religion, economic status or ethnic background, is that deep down inside, we all believe that we are above average drivers."*
– Author Dave Barry,
*16 Things It Took Me Over 50 Years To Learn*

When you look at your investments in terms of income production during retirement, you may find that you have a different level of risk tolerance than you did during your working years, when growth and accumulation were your main focus. The investments you chose to help grow your money may be different than the investments you need when relying on that money to supply your income. Reports like the Financial Overview and the Rule of

100 can help give you a good idea of where you stand now. But how do you discover allocations that can do the most to deliver the maximum income for the minimum amount of dollars? What is the safest way to grow your money during retirement, and how can you structure your income-producing investments to incur the least amount of tax burden? Like a smooth running engine, a good financial plan keeps all the parts working together to generate your income.

The title of this chapter comes from an expression in the military long ago adopted by the racing community. Moving fast or rushing during battle leads to reckless decisions and will likely get you killed. If you move slowly, with care and focused deliberateness, however, you are really moving as fast as you can without needlessly increasing the risk. In racing, when your focus is on achieving a smooth ride, you'll naturally go faster as a result. Focusing only on speed, or pushing too hard, is reckless and will likely cause you to break the car or crash. You can't get to the finish line if that happens. This difference can be compared to risk during retirement.

Volatility in the stock market refers to its tendency to vary, meaning it moves up and down within a given time period. This type of movement increases your risk because you can't know with certainty whether or not the money will be there when you need it. This is not conducive to a smooth ride during retirement. Even if you feel that you have plenty of money in your 401(k) or IRA, not knowing how much risk those investments are exposed to can cause you major financial suffering. Take the market crash of 2008 for example. In 2008, the average investor lost 30 percent of their 401(k). If more people had shifted their investments away from risk as they neared retirement age (i.e. the Rule of 100), they may have lost a lot less money going into retirement. The more risk you can remove or mitigate, the smoother (and faster) your ride will be and the less likely you are to run out of money before you make it to the finish line.

Removing the obstacles to a smooth ride begins with a careful examination of your Hope So and Know So Money. In our first meeting, we learn about your goals and what assets you have. In our second meeting, we take a look at those assets and evaluate them based on how well they are helping you achieve your goals. Assigning colors to your Hope So and Know So investments allows you to create a visual schematic so you can view your portfolio in terms of risk and potential loss.

## THE COLOR OF MONEY

To explain why certain investments are better suited for income production than others, it can be helpful to assign colors according to the amount of risk the investment is exposed to. For our purposes, Know So Money (which is safer and more dependable) is green. Hope So Money (which is exposed to risk and fluctuates with the market) is red. A financial professional can help you better understand the color of the money in your investment portfolio.

The fact of the matter is that a lot of people don't know their level of exposure to risk. Visually organizing your assets is an important and powerful way to get a clear picture of what kind of money you have, where it is and how you can best use it in the future. This process is as simple as listing your assets and assigning

| Green Money | Red Money | Yellow Money |
|---|---|---|
| "Green Money" is safer. | "Red Money" is at risk. | "Yellow Money" is Red Money that is professionally managed with a purpose. |
| This is money that offers a minimum guarantee but it may pose risks other than market risk. | This is money that can go up or down in value. It may pose risk if it is not properly managed to serve a specific purpose in a comprehensive plan. | Its risk is mitigated because it is properly managed to serve a specific purpose in a comprehensive plan. |

them a color based on their status as Know So or Hope So Money. Work with your financial professional to create a comprehensive inventory of your assets to understand what you are working with before making any decisions. This may be the first time you have ever sat down and sorted out all of your assets, allowing you to see how much money you have at risk in the market. Comparing the color of your investments will give you an idea of how near or far you are from adhering to the Rule of 100.

Over the course of your lifetime, it is likely that you have acquired a variety of assets. Assets can range from money that you have in a savings account or a 401(k), to a pension or an IRA. You have earned money and have made financial decisions based on the best information you had at the time. When viewed as a whole, however, you might not have an overall strategy for the management of your assets. As we have seen, it's more important than ever to know which of your assets are at risk. High market volatility and low treasury rates make for challenging financial topography. Navigating this financial landscape starts with planful asset management that takes into account your specific needs and options.

The next step is to know the right amount and ratio of Green and Red Money for you at your stage of retirement planning.

Investing heavily in Red Money and gambling all of your assets on the market is incredibly risky no matter where you fall within the Rule of 100. Money in the market can't be depended on to generate income, and a plan that leans too heavily on Red Money can easily fail, especially when investment decisions are influenced by emotional reactions to market downturns and recoveries. Not only is this an unwise plan, it can be incredibly stressful to an investor who is gambling everything on stocks and mutual funds.

But a plan that uses too much Green Money avoids all volatility and can also fail. Why? Investing all of your money in Certificates of Deposit (CDs), savings accounts, money markets and other low return accounts may provide interest and income, but that likely won't be enough to keep pace with inflation. If you focus exclusively on income from Green Money and avoid owning any stocks or mutual funds in your portfolio, you won't be able to leverage the potential for long-term growth your portfolio needs to stay healthy and productive. This is where the Rule of 100 can help you determine how much of your money should be invested in the market to anticipate your future needs.

Green Money becomes much more important as you age. While you want to reduce the amount of Red Money you have and to transition it to Green Money, you don't necessarily need all of it to generate income for you right away. Taking a closer look at Green Money, you will see there are actually different types.

## TYPES OF GREEN MONEY:
### *NEED NOW AND NEED LATER*
Money that you need to depend on for income is Green Money. Once you have filled the income gap at the beginning of your retirement, you may have money left over.

*There are two types of Green Money:* money used for income and money used for accumulation to meet your income needs in five, 10 or 20 years. Money needed for income is Need Now Money. It is money you need to meet your basic needs, to pay your bills, your mortgage if you have one and the costs associated with maintaining your lifestyle. Money used for accumulation is Need Later Money. It's money that you don't need now for income, but will need to rely on down the road. It's still Green Money because you will rely on it later for income and will need to count on it being there. Need Later Money represents income your assets will need to generate for future use. When planning your retirement, it is vital to decide how much of your assets to structure for income and how much to set aside to accumulate to create Need Later Money.

You must figure out if your income and accumulation needs are met. Your Need Now and Need Later Money are top priorities. Need Now Money, in particular, will dictate what your options for future needs are.

## THE RETIREMENT COMPASS: OPTIMIZING INCOME

One way to help determine your Need Now and Need Later Money needs is with the help of a computer-generated report known as The Retirement Compass. This nifty report takes a look at where you will get your income from during retirement. It analyzes your current investments, looks at your current Green Money sources of income such as Social Security benefits and pensions payments, and makes recommendations.

The report uses your asset base and recommends income vehicles to show you how much income you will have and for how long. Some income sources will run out, while other sources will be there forever. The Retirement Compass is a pretty cool tool that can help you dial in to where you should be with regard to income production. It shows you what percentage of your Red Money to reallocate to Green Money in order to reduce or eliminate risk to your lifestyle.

» *Catherine was thinking about retiring in five years, and she had a small but respectable 401(k) plan. The money from her 401(k) and her Social Security was all she had to rely on for income during retirement. She was worried about the safety of her 401(k), but she was also worried about running out of money during retirement. She thought she needed to stay in the market and keep her savings at risk in order to grow enough money. After running a Retirement Compass Report, Catherine saw that she had 95 percent of her savings in Red Money investments. The compass recommended that she move 50 percent of this money into a Green Money invest-*

*ment. To her great surprise, **Catherine** discovered that the Green Money investment, combined with her Social Security benefit, generated a lifetime stream of guaranteed income that she would never outlive. **Catherine** was able to meet her retirement goals without any risk to her income while utilizing a different strategy to grow her remaining funds for Need Later Money needs.*

## WHAT CAN GO WRONG?

A lot of retirees are surprised to learn that there are viable alternatives to the traditional ways of investing. Given the uncertainty of a global economy, it is of utmost importance that they take charge of their asset allocation and understand their options.

The biggest mistake you can make upon entering retirement is to keep your money invested in accumulation mode, relying on market investments such as stocks and mutual funds for your income. A lot of retirees are told by their brokers that if they keep their money in the market and follow some kind of withdrawal formula—usually anywhere from 4 to 6 percent—without taking money from their principal, then they will be just fine. The problem with this kind of income plan is that it does nothing to protect you against the risk of things going wrong. Consider the following "what if" scenarios and ask yourself, what are the chances?

**What if the market takes another downturn?** Since the year 1900, we have had 22 recessions, or approximately one recession every five to six years.* Given that your investments need to produce an average of at least 20 years of income, what are the chances that your assets would survive another recession like the

---

* *National Bureau of Economic Research. US Business Cycle Expansions and Contractions. http://www.nber.org/cycles.html*

one we saw in 2008? What are your chances of surviving four recessions?

**What if I get sick and need long-term care?** One of the biggest risks during retirement is having to access funds during a down market. If you are experiencing an illness and have to withdraw additional money during a market downturn, it can be catastrophic to the durability of your income plan. Almost 70 percent of all people turning age 65 will need some form of long-term care during their lives.* Long-term care refers to a wide range of services, many of which have less to do with getting sick and more to do with our body's natural decline. The U.S. Department of Health and Human Services reports that most people using long-term care need help with basic personal tasks such as bathing or getting up from a chair. As we age, our bodies get tired and it simply becomes harder to do the things we normally do. These activities are known as ADLs, or the six Activities of Daily Living, and they include the following:

- Eating
- Bathing
- Getting dressed
- Using the bathroom
- Transferring (moving to or from a bed or chair)
- Caring for incontinence

While purchasing traditional long-term care insurance protects your assets should you or your spouse get sick, these types of policies can be expensive. As you get older, they become more and more difficult to qualify for and fund. Perhaps the biggest downside to this solution is the fact that any money paid into the policy is surrendered to the insurance company should you

---

*U.S. Department of Health and Human Services <http://longtermcare.gov/the-basics/>*

never need long-term care. If you'd rather not put your money in something you may never use, a long-term care rider purchased with an annuity product might be a more attractive solution.

You get to control how the money is spent, either to fund in-home care, assisted living or more comprehensive medical care in a nursing home. Perhaps the most attractive feature of this solution is that should you never get sick or never need long-term care, any remaining money in your policy is paid out to your beneficiaries. This means the money invested is never lost.

## ARE YOU DRIVING A CAR WITHOUT HEADLIGHTS?

It can be hard to know who to trust these days when it comes to advice about money. While no one will ever care more about your money than you do, when looking for advice and guidance about the allocation of your retirement assets, it's important to understand the legal standards your financial professional is held to. The motivation behind the advice given can be best understood by looking at the difference between suitability and fiduciary standards.

**Suitability standards dictate that your financial professional can sell you a product as long as it is considered suitable, even though the product might not necessarily be the best fit for your needs.**

To help illustrate this point, let's use another racing metaphor. Readers with grandkids may be familiar with the rookie racecar, Lightning McQueen, from the Disney film, *Cars*. McQueen was a race car designed to race on a track. As such, he had no brake lights and no headlights. In place of those lights, race cars have stickers because in the world of NASCAR, the tracks are always lit. Off-road racing is another kind of racing altogether. When competing long-distance across rough terrain, such as the Baja 1,000 off-road desert race, headlights are an absolute must.

Without them, you run the risk of driving straight off a cliff in the middle of the night.

Now let's say you are in the market for a race car that can carry you all the way through retirement. If you knew nothing at all about race cars, you might not realize that an off-road vehicle would be your best option, given that retirement is a long race. If you went to a professional held to suitability standards and told them, "I need a race car," they would recommend a vehicle from their selection of NASCAR racers designed to perform best on a track, because those are the only kinds of cars they have in stock. They wouldn't have access to other vehicles, and they wouldn't have to take the time to understand your situation, either, such as why you need the car and where you are going. The race car they sell you could be considered a "suitable" vehicle, even though it has no headlights and no suspension and will likely get you into a great deal of trouble when the sun sets and you realize your headlights are nothing but a pair of stickers.

No one wants to spend their retirement driving around in the dark. It's pretty obvious when you've made a mistake about your choice of automobile, but with investments, mistakes might not show up until several miles (or years) down the road. This is where fiduciary standards come in to play.

**Operating under fiduciary standards, financial professionals are obligated to act in good faith and with candor, to be proactive in disclosing any conflicts of interest that may impact a client, and to make recommendations that are always in the client's best interest.**

The National Association of Personal Financial Advisors (NAPFA) describes financial professionals held to fiduciary standards as a occupying a position of special trust and confidence when working with a client, because they are required to act with undivided loyalty.* An investment advisor held to fiduciary standards strives to:

- Put your interests first.
- Understand your specific financial situation.
- Offer straightforward advice that reflects your long-term goals.
- Recommend investment solutions that best fit your unique needs.

If you went to a professional held to fiduciary standards and told them you needed a racecar, they would ask you several questions first before recommending any vehicles. After learning that you want a racecar for a long-distance off-road race, this professional would be legally obligated to help you find the best off-road racing vehicle out there with your budget in mind. This is why a fiduciary professional spends time to get to know you first, before they begin advising about which investment vehicles can best serve you.

Working with a Registered Investment Advisor means working with a professional who is legally obligated to help you make financial decisions that are in your best interest and fall within your comfort zone. Taking steps toward creating a retirement plan is nothing to take lightly. By leveraging tax strategies, properly organizing your assets, and accumulating helpful financial vehicles that help you meet your income and accumulation needs, you are more likely to meet your goals. You might have a million dollars socked away in a savings account, but your neighbor, who has $300,000 in a diverse investment portfolio that is tailored to their needs, may end up enjoying a better retirement lifestyle. Why? They had more than a good work ethic and a penchant for saving. They had a planning-first approach to retirement asset allocation.

---

* *http://www.napfa.org/about/FiduciaryOath.asp*

## CHAPTER 2 RECAP //

- There are two types of money: Green and Red. Green Money represents assets that are "safer" and more reliable. Red Money represents assets that are exposed to risk.
- There are two types of Green Money: *Need Now and Need Later*. It is important to structure your investments to provide you with income now and later.
- Understand the source of the investment advice you are given. A professional held to fiduciary standards is legally bound to recommend products that are in your best interest. A professional held to suitability standards is not prohibited from recommending products that pay out the highest fees to him or her, as long as those products are "suitable." Suitability isn't wrong; it just may not be the best fit for retirees.

# 3

# HOW FAR DO YOU
# WANT TO GO?

*"After the third flip, I lost control..."*
– Don Roberts after crashing in the Jade Grenada
at New England Dragway in 1925

An important aspect of your financial plan is the evaluation of your income needs. Finding the most efficient and beneficial way to address them will have impacts on your lifestyle, your asset accumulation and your legacy planning after you retire. When you have identified your income need, you will know how much to structure for income and how much to be set aside for accumulation.

***Every financial strategy for retirement needs first to accommodate the day-to-day need for income.*** The moment your working income ceases and you start living off the money you've set aside for retirement is referred to as the **retirement cliff**. When you begin drawing income from your retirement assets, you have entered the distribution phase of your financial plan. *The distribution phase of your retirement plan* is when you reach the point of relying on your assets for income. This is where your Green Money comes into play: the safer, more reliable assets that you have accumulated that are designed to provide you with a steady income. On day one of your retirement, you will need a steady and reliable supply of income from your Green Money.

Satisfying that need for daily income entails first knowing *how much you need* and *when you will need it.*

» *Ben and Karen were ready to retire. They had a $500,000 IRA invested in mutual funds with their stockbroker, and they had some other stocks they inherited from Ben's father. They felt pretty good about the amount of assets they had to rely on, but they were still concerned about running out of money. They decided to make an appointment with a financial professional to get advice about income planning.*

*When they sat down with the professional, he asked them, "Has your current broker done an income plan for you? Do you have a number?"*

*"Oh yes," Ben says. "Our number is 6 percent. He says as long as we average 6 percent a year in our investments, we'll be fine."*

*"Okay, well, that's not the number I had in mind, but we can start there. There is a flaw in that thinking."*

*Ben and Karen looked at each other. "A flaw?" they asked in unison.*

*"Yes. Retirement can last a long time. Is the stock market going to go up 6 percent every year for the rest of your life? Probably not. The market is going to go up, and it's going to go down. When it goes down, that's disastrous for someone*

*during retirement. Using that number as an income strategy puts you at risk of running out of money in about ten years, even though you've done an excellent job of saving."*

*The financial professional went on to show them a phenomenon known as the Sequence of Returns. Ben and Karen had an "ah-ha moment." They began to understand the rate of growth on their investments isn't as important as the timing of the up and down cycle, and they have no control over that timing. (To read more about the Sequence of Returns, see Chapter 6).*

*Ben and Karen had no idea they had other options. Their financial professional showed them how to create an income plan so they didn't need to take on risk during retirement.*

## CREATING AN INCOME PLAN

The most essential element to retirement planning is the ability of your savings to provide you with the income you need. Your savings and the assets you have accumulated in combination with your Social Security and other benefits are the resource for creating this income. Creating an income plan using the old rules based on a rate of return is like driving a car without headlights along the retirement highway. This kind of income plan is disastrous to anyone during retirement who wants their money to last as long as they do.

You first want to ask yourself, *how much income do I need?* Taking the time to design an income plan based on your needs means you won't have to take on unnecessary risk during your retirement. When you know how much money you need, you can then transition a portion of your assets into a Know So investment vehicle designed to meet your income needs without the fear of risk.

Take a moment to evaluate your daily income needs and retirement goals.

- What is your lifestyle today?
- Would you like to maintain it into retirement?
- Are you meeting your needs?
- Are you happy with your lifestyle?
- What do you really *need* to live on when you retire?

Some people will have the luxury of maintaining or improving their lifestyle, while others may have to make decisions about what they need versus what they want during their retirement. Once you have identified your income need, you will know what percentage of Green Money investments to structure for income and how much to set aside for accumulation needs down the road.

## HOW MUCH AND WHEN?

How Much Money Do You Need? While this amount will be different for everyone, the general rule of thumb is that a retiree will require 70 to 80 percent of their pre-retirement income to maintain their lifestyle. Once you know what that number is, the key becomes matching your income need with the correct investment strategies, options and tools to satisfy that need.

**When Do You Need Your Money?** If you need income to last 10 years, use a tool that creates just that. If you need a lifetime of income, seek a tool that will do that and won't run out. There are new indexed annuity vehicles available that are designed to address the longevity concerns of today's retirees. These products provide protection of principal with growth and a guaranteed income stream for life, no matter how long you live. We will talk about how to use investment vehicles for income creation in Chapter 5.

So how do you figure out how much you need and when you need it? When you take health care costs, potential emergencies, plans for moving or traveling, and other retirement expenses into account, you can really give your calculator a workout. You want to maximize retirement benefits to meet your lifetime income needs. An Investment Advisor can help you answer those questions by working with you to customize an income plan. One of the most important things they can help you address is the structuring of your first legacy: how you and your spouse will take care of each other.

## YOUR FIRST LEGACY

When competing in a 1,000 mile off-road race, you work with a race crew. Each member of the team is responsible for driving a certain section of the race or chasing the race and fixing the car if it breaks. When you arrive at your checkpoint, you want the car to be in good enough condition to carry your teammate onward to the next checkpoint. This brings up two salient points:

1. Everyone in the retirement race with you needs to know how to operate the investment vehicles just like every racer and team needs to know how to drive the car, fix the car, and operate the GPS system.

2. You want to maintain your vehicle in an appropriate manner, which means properly structuring your assets so you don't make the mistake of leaving your spouse walking down the highway instead of riding down the highway.

Your first legacy is the one that you leave for your spouse. You want to make sure the person you love is taken care of in the event of your death. Poverty after the loss of a spouse is more common among women than men.* Many women find they have fewer options of guaranteed income sources, or they simply don't know how to drive the racecar of their husband's investments. You can avoid this by taking the time now to understand your investment

---

* *http://www.ssa.gov/policy/docs/ssb/v65n3/v65n3p31.html*

options so when the hard times come, you're prepared and have a solid plan to follow.

When one spouse passes, there is usually loss of income, either in the form of a Social Security benefit check, a pension, or both. There are investment vehicles designed to provide spousal continuation, offering a joint-life income option so both spouses are protected against income loss. Still other couples choose to set aside a separate account with an income rider that is allowed to grow and isn't turned on until the money is needed.

Regardless of what option you choose, it's important for both spouses to be involved in the income planning process. If your husband or wife handles all the accounts, make sure you understand how much income will be coming if he or she passes away. Also, find out whether or not that income comes from a guaranteed source.

As we determined earlier in Chapter 1, the most important thing you need to do as you create an income plan is to take care to avoid too much exposure to risk. You can start by meeting with an Investment Advisor to organize your assets. Get your Green Money and Red Money in order and balanced to meet your needs. If the market goes down 18 percent this afternoon, you don't want that to come out of what you're relying on for next year's income.

Hot on the heels of securing your Green Money, it's time to structure those Green Money assets so they can generate income for you. Ultimately, you have to take care of your monthly income needs to pay the bills. The Big Kahuna of Green Money is your Social Security benefit.

## CHAPTER 3 RECAP //

- The foundation of a retirement strategy depends on knowing how much money you need and when you need it.
- The first legacy you leave is to your spouse. Spousal continuation is one area often overlooked during income planning. When one spouse dies, the loss of pensions and monetary benefits such as Social Security means a reduction in monthly income. Your income plan should take into consideration guaranteed sources of income that will still be available after your spouse passes away.

# 4

# YOUR PRIMARY PARACHUTE: SOCIAL SECURITY

*"Just because no one complains, it doesn't mean*
*100 percent of the parachutes are working."*
— Benny Hill

One kind of Green Money that most Americans can rely on for income when they retire is Social Security. If you're like most Americans, Social Security is or will be an important part of your retirement income. You might even think of it as your primary parachute, which is why it's important to understand how and when to deploy this lifetime benefit. As a first step in creating your income plan, a financial professional will take a look at your Social Security benefit options. Social Security is the foundation of income planning for anyone who is about to retire and is a reliable source of Green Money in your overall income plan.

> *Kristine had worked full-time nearly her entire adult life and was looking forward to enjoying retirement with her husband, kids and grandkids. When she turned 62, she decided to take advantage of her Social Security benefits as soon as they became available.*
>
> *A couple of years later, she was organizing some of the paperwork in her home office. She came across an old Social Security statement, and remembered the feeling of filing and beginning a new phase in her life.*
>
> *However, as she looked over the statement, she realized in retrospect that she might have been better off waiting to file for benefits. She had saved enough to wait for benefits, and if she had, her monthly benefit could have been quite a bit more.*
>
> *When she was in the process of retiring, there were so many other decisions to make. It seemed very straightforward to file right away. She made a note to call the Social Security Administration to see if it was possible to change her monthly benefit to the larger amount.*

Here are some facts that illustrate how Americans currently use Social Security:

- Nearly 90 percent of Americans age 65 and older receive Social Security benefits.*
- Social Security provides about 39 percent of the income of the elderly.*

---

* *http://www.ssa.gov/pressoffice/basicfact.htm*

- Claiming Social Security benefits at the wrong time can reduce your monthly benefit by up to 65 percent.*
- In 2013, 36 percent of men and 40 percent of women claimed Social Security benefits at age 62.**
- In 2013, more than a third of workers claimed Social Security benefits as soon they became eligible.**
- In 2015, the average monthly Social Security benefit was $1,328. *The maximum benefit for 2015 was $2,663. The $1,335 monthly benefit reduction between the average and the maximum is applied for life.****

There are many aspects of Social Security that are well known and others that aren't. When it comes time for you to cash in on your Social Security benefit, you will have many options and choices. Social Security is a massive government program that manages retirement benefits for millions of people. Experts spend their entire careers understanding and analyzing it. Luckily, you don't have to understand all of the intricacies of Social Security to maximize its advantages. You simply need to know the best way to manage your Social Security benefit. You need to know exactly what to do to get the most from your Social Security benefit and when to do it. Taking the time to create a roadmap for your Social Security strategy will help ensure that you are able to exact your maximum benefit and efficiently coordinate it with the rest of your retirement plan.

There are many aspects of Social Security that you have no control over. You don't control how much you put into it, and

---

* https://www.ssa.gov/planners/retire/retirechart.html

** Trends in Social Security Claiming, Alicia H Munnell and Anqi Chen, Center for Retirement Research, May 2015. http://crr.bc.edu/wp-content/uploads/2015/05/IB_15-8.pdf

*** https://www.ssa.gov/news/press/factsheets/colafacts2015.html

you don't control what it's invested in or how the government manages it. However, you do control when and how you file for benefits. The real question about Social Security that you need to answer is, "When should I start taking Social Security?" While this is the all-important question, there are a couple of key pieces of information you need to track down first.

Before we get into a few calculations and strategies that can make all the difference, let's start by covering the basic information about Social Security which should give you an idea of where you stand. Just as the foundation of a house creates the stable platform for the rest of the framework to rest upon, your Social Security benefit is an important part of your overall retirement plan. The purpose of the information that follows is not to give an exhaustive explanation of how Social Security works, but to give you some tools and questions to start understanding how Social Security affects your retirement and how you can prepare for it.

Let's start with eligibility.

**Eligibility.** Understanding how and when you are eligible for Social Security benefits will help clarify what to expect when the time comes to claim them.

To receive retirement benefits from Social Security, you must earn eligibility. In almost all cases, Americans born after 1929 must earn 40 quarters of credit to be eligible to draw their Social Security retirement benefit. In 2015, a Social Security credit represents $1,220 earned in a calendar quarter. The number changes as it is indexed each year, but not drastically. In 2014, a credit represented $1,200. Four quarters of credit is the maximum number that can be earned each year. In 2015, an American would have had to earn at least $4,880 to accumulate four credits. In order to qualify for retirement benefits, you must have earned a minimum number of credits. Additionally, if you are at least 62 years old and have been married to a recipient of Social Security benefits for at least 12 months, you can choose to receive Spousal Benefits. Although 40 is the minimum number of credits required to begin drawing benefits, it is important to know that once you claim your Social Security benefit, there is no going back. Although there may be cost of living adjustments made, you are locked into that base benefit amount forever.

**Primary Insurance Amount.** You can think of your Primary Insurance Amount (PIA) like a ripening fruit. It represents the amount of your Social Security benefit at your Full Retirement Age (FRA). Your benefit becomes fully ripe at your FRA, and will neither reduce nor increase due to early or delayed retirement options. If you opt to take benefits before your FRA, however, your monthly benefit will be less than your PIA. You will essentially be picking an unripe fruit. On the one hand, waiting until after your FRA to access your benefits will increase your benefit beyond your PIA. On the other hand, you don't want the fruit to become overripe, because every month you wait is one less check you get from the government.

**Full Retirement Age.** Your FRA is an important figure for anyone who is planning to rely on Social Security benefits in their retirement. Depending on when you were born, there is a specific age at which you will attain FRA. Your FRA is dictated by your year of birth and is the age at which you can begin receiving your full monthly benefit. Your FRA is important because it is half of the equation used to calculate your Social Security benefit. The other half of the equation is based on when you start taking benefits

When Social Security was initially set up, the FRA was age 65, and it still is for people born before 1938. But as time has passed, the age for receiving full retirement benefits has increased. If you were born between 1938 and 1960, your full retirement age is somewhere on a sliding scale between 65 and 67. Anyone born in

1960 or later will now have to wait until age 67 for full benefits. Increasing the FRA has helped the government reduce the cost of the Social Security program, which paid out almost $870 billion to beneficiaries in 2015!*

While you can begin collecting benefits as early as age 62, the amount you receive as a monthly benefit will be less than it would be if you wait until you reach or surpass your FRA. It is important to note that if you file for your Social Security benefit before your FRA, *the reduction to your monthly benefit will remain in place for the rest of your life.* You can also delay receiving benefits up to age 70, in which case your benefits will be higher than your PIA for the rest of your life.

- At FRA, 100 percent of PIA is available as a monthly benefit.
- At age 62, your Social Security retirement benefits are available. For each month you take benefits prior to your FRA, however, the monthly amount of your benefit is reduced. *This reduction stays in place for the rest of your life.*
- At age 70, your monthly benefit reaches its maximum. After you turn age 70, your monthly benefit will no longer increase.

| Year of Birth | Full Retirement Age |
|---|---|
| 1943-1954 | 66 |
| 1955 | 66 and 2 months |
| 1956 | 66 and 4 months |
| 1957 | 66 and 6 months |
| 1958 | 66 and 8 months |
| 1959 | 66 and 10 months |
| 1960 or later | age 67** |

---

* https://www.ssa.gov/news/press/basicfact.html

** http://www.ssa.gov/OACT/progdata/nra.html

## ROLLING UP YOUR SOCIAL SECURITY

Your Social Security income "rolls up" the longer you wait to claim it. Your monthly benefit will continue to increase until you turn 70 years old. Even though Social Security is the foundation of most people's retirement, many Americans feel that they don't have control over how or when they receive their benefits. The truth is that every dollar you increase your Social Security income by means less money you will have to spend from your nest egg to meet your retirement income needs, but many retirees do not take advantage of this fact. For many people, creating their Social Security strategy is the most important decision they can make to positively impact their retirement. *The difference between the best and worst Social Security decision can be tens of thousands of dollars over a lifetime of benefits.*

**Deciding NOW or** LATER: Following the above logic, it makes sense to wait as long as you can to begin receiving your Social Security benefit. However, the answer isn't always that simple. Not everyone has the option of waiting. Many people need to rely on Social Security on day one of their retirement. Some might need the income. Others might be in poor health and don't feel they will live long enough to make waiting until their FRA worthwhile for themselves or their families. It is also possible, however, that the majority of folks taking an early benefit at age 62 are simply under-informed about Social Security. Perhaps they make this major decision based on rumors and emotion.

**File Immediately if You:**
- Find your job is unbearable.
- Are willing to sacrifice retirement income.
- Are not healthy and need a reliable source of income.

**Consider Delaying Your Benefit if You:**
- Want to maximize your retirement income.
- Want to increase retirement benefits for your spouse.
- Are still working and like it.
- Are healthy and willing / able to wait to file.

So if you decide to wait, how long should you wait? Lots of people can put it off for a few years, but not everyone can wait until they are 70 years old. Your individual circumstances may be able to help you determine when you should begin taking Social Security. If you do the math, you will quickly see that between ages 62 and 70, there are 96 months in which you can file for your Social Security benefit. If you take into account those 96 months and the 96 months your spouse could also file for Social Security, and the number of different strategies for structuring your benefit, you can easily end up with more than 20,000 different scenarios. It's safe to say this isn't the kind of math that most people can easily handle. Each month would result in a different benefit amount. The longer you wait, the higher your monthly benefit amount becomes. Each month you wait, however, is one less month that you receive a Social Security check.

*The goal is to maximize your lifetime benefits.* That may not always mean waiting until you can get the largest monthly payment. Taking the bigger picture into account, you want to find out how to get the most money out of Social Security over the number of years that you draw from it. Don't underestimate the power of optimizing your benefit: the difference between the BEST and WORST Social Security election can easily be worth thousands of dollars in lifetime benefits. *The difference can be very substantial!*

If you know that every month you wait, your Social Security benefit goes up a little bit, and you also know that every month you wait, you receive one less benefit check, how do you determine where the sweet spot is that maximizes your benefits over your lifetime? Financial professionals have access to software that will calculate the best year and month for you to file for benefits based on your default life expectancy. You can further customize that information by estimating your life expectancy based on your health, habits and family history. If you can then create an income plan (we'll get into this later in the chapter) that helps you wait until the target date for you to file for Social Security, you can optimize your retirement income strategy to get the most out of your Social Security benefit. How can you calculate your life expectancy? Well, you don't know exactly how long you'll live, but you have a better idea than the government does. They rely on averages to make their calculations. *You have much more personal information about your health, lifestyle and family history than they do.* You can use that knowledge to game the system and beat all the other people who are making uninformed decisions by filing early for Social Security.

While you can and should educate yourself about how Social Security works, the reality is you don't need to know a lot of general information about Social Security in order to make choices about your retirement. What you do need to know is exactly *what to do to maximize your benefit.* Because knowing what you need to do has huge impacts on your retirement! For most Americans, Social Security is the foundation of income planning for retirement. Social Security benefits represent about 39 percent of the income of the elderly.* For many people, it can represent the largest portion of their retirement income. Not treating your Social Security benefit as an asset and investment tool can lead to sub-optimization of your largest source of retirement income.

Let's take a look at an example that shows the impact of working with a financial professional to optimize Social Security benefits:

---

* *http://www.socialsecurity.gov/pressoffice/basicfact.htm*

» *Bob and Elaine Bailey are a typical American couple who have worked their whole lives and saved when they could. Greg is 60 years old, and Elaine is 56 years old. They sat down with a financial professional who logged onto the Social Security website to look up their PIAs. George's PIA is $1,900 and Mary's is $900.*

*If the Baileys cash in at age 62 and begin taking retirement benefits from Social Security, they will receive an estimated $568,600 in lifetime benefits. That may seem like a lot, but if you divide that amount over 20 years, it averages out to around $28,400 per year. The Baileys are accustomed to a more significant annual income than that. To make up the difference, they will have to rely on alternative retirement income options. They will basically have to depend on a bigger nest egg to provide them with the income they need.*

*If they wait until their FRA, they will increase their lifetime benefits to an estimated $609,000. This option allows them to achieve their Primary Insurance Amount, which will provide them a $34,200 annual income.*

*After learning the Baileys' needs and using software to calculate the most optimal time to begin drawing benefits, the Baileys' financial professional determined that the best option for them drastically increases their potential lifetime benefits to $649,000!*

*By using strategies that their financial professional recommended, they increased their potential lifetime benefits by as much as **$80,000**. There's no telling how much you could miss out on from your Social Security if you don't take time to create a strategy that calculates your maximum benefit. For the Baileys, the value of maximizing their benefits was the difference between night and day. While this may seem like a special case, it isn't uncommon to find benefit increases of this* *magnitude. You'll never know unless you take a look at your own options.*

Despite the importance of knowing when and how to take your Social Security benefit, many of today's retirees and pre-retirees may know little about the mechanics of Social Security and how they can maximize their benefit.

So, to whom should you turn for advice when making this complex decision? Before you pick up the phone and call Uncle Sam, you should know that the Social Security Administration (SSA) representatives are actually prohibited from giving you election advice! Plus, SSA representatives in general are trained to focus on monthly benefit amounts, not the lifetime income for a family.

## MAXIMIZING YOUR LIFETIME BENEFIT

As discussed in Chapter 2, calculating how to maximize **lifetime benefits** is more important than waiting until age 70 for your maximum **monthly benefit amount.** It's about getting the most income during your lifetime. Professional benefit maximization software can target the year and month that it is most beneficial for you to file based on your life expectancy.

The three most common ages that people associate with retirement benefits are 62 (Earliest Eligible Age), 66 (Full Retirement Age), and 70 (age at which monthly maximum benefit is reached). In almost all circumstances, however, none of those three most common ages will give you the maximum lifetime benefit.

Remember, every month you wait to file, the amount of your benefit check goes up, but you also get one less check. You don't know how exactly how long you're going to live, but you have a better idea of your life expectancy than the actuaries at the Social Security Administration who can only work with averages. They can't make calculations based on your specific situation. A professional can run the numbers for you and get the target date that maximizes your potential lifetime benefits. You can't get this information from the SSA, but you **can** get it from a financial professional.

**Types of Social Security Benefits:**
- *Retired Worker Benefit.* This is the benefit with which most people are familiar. The Retired Worker Benefit is what most people are talking about when they refer to Social Security. It is your benefit based on your earnings and the amount that you have paid into the system over the span of your career.
- *Spousal Benefit.* This is available to the spouse of someone who is eligible for Retired Worker Benefits.
- *Survivorship Benefit.* When one spouse passes away, the survivor is able to receive the larger of the two benefit amounts.
- *Restricted Application.* A higher-earning spouse may be able to start collecting a spousal benefit on the lower-earning spouse's benefit while allowing his or her benefit to continue to grow. Due to the Bipartisan Budget Act of 2015, this option is only available to individuals who turned age 62 before January 1, 2016.

In November of 2015, the Bipartisan Budget Act of 2015 was passed, which will have a dramatic impact on the way many Americans plan for Social Security. As the largest change to Social Security since 2000, the Bipartisan Budget Act of 2015 eliminated an estimated $9.5 billion* of benefits to retirees and may

---

* *http://www.nasdaq.com/article/congress-planning-to-close-social-security-loopholes-cm536252*

limit some of the flexibility you previously had to structure your benefits.

In 2000, Congress passed the Senior Citizens Freedom to Work Act. The bill allowed retirees to suspend receiving benefits so they wouldn't be subject to additional taxation if they chose to return to work after they filed for Social Security. However, by doing so, the bill also unintentionally created several loopholes in claiming strategies: most notably, the Restricted Application for spousal benefits and "file and suspend" filing strategy. For most Americans, the Bipartisan Budget Act of 2015 closed these loopholes by eliminating "file and suspend" and the Restricted Application.

The new rules mandate that:

- If a primary worker is not currently receiving benefits, then their dependents (child, spouse) can no longer collect benefits based on the primary worker's earning record.
- If you file for benefits, then you are filing for *all* benefits to which you are entitled—not just the benefit type you choose.

It's important to remember that in spite of these immense changes, one thing stayed the same—filing for Social Security is one of the most important financial decisions you will make in your lifetime, and a financial professional can help ensure you make the right one.

## THE DIVORCE FACTOR

How does a divorced spouse qualify for benefits? If you have gone through a divorce, it might affect the retirement benefit to which you are entitled.

In general, a person can receive benefits as a divorced spouse on a former spouse's Social Security record so long as the following conditions are met:

- the marriage lasted at least 10 years; and
- the person filing for divorce benefits is at least age 62, unmarried, and not entitled to a higher Social Security benefit on his or her own record.*

With all of the different options, strategies and benefits to choose from, you can see why filing for Social Security is more complicated than just mailing in the paperwork. Gathering the data and making yourself aware of all your different options isn't enough to know exactly what to do, however. On the one hand, you can knock yourself out trying to figure out which options are best for you and wondering if you made the best decision. On the other hand, you can work with a financial professional who uses customized software that takes all the variables of your specific situation into account and calculates your best option. You have tens of thousands of different options for filing for your Social Security benefit. If your spouse is a different age than you are, it nearly doubles the amount of options you have. This is far more complicated arithmetic than most people can do on their own. If you want a truly accurate understanding of when and how to file, you need someone who will ask you the right questions about your situation, someone who has access to specialized software that can crunch the numbers. The reality is that you need to work with a professional that can provide you with the sophisticated analysis of your situation that will help you make a truly informed decision.

**Important Questions about Your Social Security Benefit:**
- *How can I maximize my lifetime benefit?* By knowing when and how to file for Social Security. This usually means waiting until you have at least reached your Full Retire-

---

* *http://www.ssa.gov/retire2/yourdivspouse.htm*

ment Age. A professional has the experience and the tools to help determine when and how you can maximize your lifetime benefits.

- *Who will provide reliable advice for making these decisions?* Only a professional has the tools and experience to provide you reliable advice.

- *Will the Social Security Administration provide me with the advice?* The Social Security Administration cannot provide you with advice or strategies for claiming your benefit. They can give you information about your monthly benefit, but that's it. They also don't have the tools to tell you what your specific best option is. They can accurately answer how the system works, but they can't advise you on what decision to make as to how and when to file for benefits.

The Maximization Report that your financial professional will generate represents an invaluable resource for understanding how and when to file for your Social Security benefit. When you get your customized Social Security Maximization Report, you will not only know all the options available to you—but you will understand the financial implications of each choice. In addition to the analysis, you will also get a report that shows *exactly* at what age—including which month and year—you should trigger benefits and how you should apply. It also includes a variety of other time-specific recommendations, such as when to apply for Medicare or take Required Minimum Distributions from your qualified plans. A report means there is no need to wonder, or to try to figure out when to take action—the Social Security Maximization Report lays it all out for you in plain English.

## CHAPTER 4 RECAP //

- To get the most out of your Social Security benefit, you need to file at the right time.
- An Investment Advisor can help you determine when you should file for Social Security to get your Maximum Lifetime Benefit.

# 5

# INCOME VEHICLES THAT GUARANTEE A PAYCHECK FOR LIFE

*"Set peace of mind as your highest goal,
and organize your life around it."*
– Brian Tracy

The moment that you stop working and start living off the money that you've set aside for retirement can be referred to as the Retirement Cliff. You've worked and earned money your whole life, but the day that you retire, that income comes to an end. That's the day that you have to have other assets that fill the gap. Social Security will fill in some, but you need to come up with something else.

After you have calculated your Social Security benefit and have selected the year and month that will maximize your lifetime benefits, it's time to look at your other retirement assets, incomes and options that will reduce or eliminate the dropoff of the Retirement Cliff. You may have a pension, an IRA or Roth IRA, dividends from stock holdings, money from the sale of real estate, rental property, or other sources of income. What other sources of reliable income do you have?

If your monthly Social Security check and your other supplemental income leaves a shortfall in your *desired* income, how are you going to fix it? This shortfall is called the **Income Gap** and it needs to be filled in order to maintain your lifestyle into retirement. If your gap is large, then you will need to rely on a larger portion of your assets for income; if the gap is small, then you will use less. The goal is to fill that income gap with the fewest dollars possible. You basically want to buy that income gap for the least amount of money possible. You don't want it to cost you too much, because you want to get the most out of your other assets, including planning for your future health care expenses and planning for your legacy. To increase the efficiency of your savings to produce the desired amount of income, you may want to consider using an investment vehicle specifically designed for income production. Such a vehicle exists, and it's called an annuity.

## ANNUITIES: WHAT YOU HAVE HEARD AND WHY

Many people are told by their broker that annuities are horrible products and that you should never put your money in one. An annuity is an income-creating investment and as such, there is no other investment that can replace what an annuity can do. During retirement, it's all about the ability of your savings to produce income You are essentially unemployed (and hopefully enjoying it!), which is why annuities deserve a second look.

If all of this is true, then why are some people saying that annuities are horrible? Going back to our car metaphor, it helps first to remember that vehicles capable of producing income for the long term can be compared to off-road vehicles, and brokers simply don't have a large selection of off-road vehicles in stock. While a broker or registered representative can offer you variable annuities which are invested in the stock market, they cannot offer you the guaranteed types of income annuities offered by an investment advisor and discussed in this chapter. When working with a broker subject to suitability standards, the money you have in the market is working for them more reliably than it is for you. By keeping the majority of your savings in the stock market, your money is paying them an annual commission, whether the investment makes you money or not. If you take your money out of the market, you will no longer be paying the broker his commission or fees, which means he or she loses the income.

**If I could show you a way to earn interest on your taxes instead of paying taxes on your interest, would that be of value to you?** This can be accomplished with an annuity, by repositioning assets out of vehicles that are providing you with a 1099 statement and into vehicles that don't. Ask yourself the following questions:

- How concerned are you about finding a secure financial vehicle to protect your savings?
- How concerned are you that there may be a better way to structure your savings?

If you are concerned about the best way to fill your income gap, an income annuity investment tool is likely a good option for you. Income annuities have many similar qualities to Social Security that give them the same look and feel as that reliable benefit check you get every month. Most importantly, an income annuity can be an efficient and profitable way to solve your income gap.

Finding the right annuity for you will take a conversation with your financial professional. Be sure you fully understand the features, benefits and costs of any annuity you are considering before investing money.

## HOW TO GET YOUR PAYCHECK FOR LIFE

You looked at Social Security strategies earlier, discovering you have some control over how and when you file. Those decisions can change the outcome of your benefit in your favor. Once you start drawing that income, it is safer and will provide you with a reliable source of income for the rest of your life. While there are many factors of Social Security that you can control, there are many that you cannot.

For example, you do not have the choice of putting more money into Social Security in order to get more out of it. If you could have the option to contribute more money toward Social Security in order to secure a guaranteed income, it would be a great way to create a Green Money asset that would enhance your retirement. Since that option isn't available, you may seek an investment tool that is similar to Social Security that provides you with a reliable income. It also has the potential to increase the value of your principal investment! This kind of win-win situation exists, and it's called an income annuity.

### Here is how they can work:

When you put your money into an annuity, you are essentially buying an investment product from an insurance company. It is a contract between you and the insurance company that provides the investment tool. Let's say you have saved $100,000 and need it to generate income to meet your needs above and beyond your Social Security and pension checks. You give the $100,000 to an insurance company, who in turn invests it to generate growth.

They usually select investments that have modest returns over long term horizons. In other words, they generally put it somewhere stable and predictable. Most commonly, they will invest it in a combination of bonds and treasuries that are safer and dependable ways to grow money. They use the money from the insurance products they sell to invest, use a portion of the returns to generate profits for themselves, and return a portion to clients in the form of payouts, claims, and structured income options.

One of the most attractive qualities of these types of annuities is something called annual reset. Annual reset is sometimes also referred to as a "ratcheting." Instead of taking on the risk that comes with putting money in a fluctuating market, you can offset that risk onto the insurance company. It works like this: If the market goes down, you don't suffer a loss. Instead, the insurance company absorbs it. But if the market goes up, you share with the insurance company some of the profit made on the gain. The amount of gain you get is called your annuity participation rate. Typically the insurer will cap the amount of gain you can realize at somewhere between 3 and 7 percent. If the market goes up 10 percent, you would realize a portion of that gain (whatever percentage you are capped at). This means you to never lose money on your investment, while always gaining a portion of the upswings. The measurement period of your annuity can be calculated monthly, weekly and even daily, but most annuities are measured annually. The level of the index when you buy and the index level one year later will determine the amount of loss or gain. You and the insurance company are betting that the market will generally go up over time.

## THE DIFFERENCE AN INCOME RIDER CAN MAKE

When you use that $100,000 to buy a contract with an insurance company in the form of an annuity, you are pegging your money on an index. It could be the S&P 500, the Dow Jones Industrial

Average or any number of indexes. To generate income from the annuity, you select something called an income rider. An income rider is a subset of an indexed annuity. Essentially, it is the amount of money from which the insurance company will pay you an income while you have your money in their annuity. Your income rider is a larger number than what your investment is actually worth, and if you select the income rider, it will increase in value over time, providing you with more income.

**You might say that an income rider is like a backup parachute. Even if the actual value of your annuity account falls to zero, the income rider is still guaranteed to pay out your income for as long as you live.** You pay a small fee for this additional protection, but for many people it's the difference between winning in retirement and not making it to the finish line.

While this might sound too good to be true, keep in mind that insurance companies make long-term investments that provide them with predictable flows of money. They like to stabilize the amount of money that goes in and out of their doors instead of paying and receiving large unpredictable chunks at once. When you opt for an income rider, an insurance company can reliably predict how much money they will pay out to you over a set period of time. It's predictable, and they like that. They can base their business on those predictable numbers. As the insurance company holds your money and invests it, they generate a return on it that they use to pay you a regular monthly income based on a higher number. For their part, the insurance company has to outperform the amount that they pay you in order to make a profit.

The following example shows just how helpful an indexed annuity with an income rider can be for a retiree:

> » *Peter and Nikki are 62 years old and have decided to run the numbers to see what their retirement is going to look like.*

*This is a hypothetical illustration*

*They know they currently need $6,000 per month to pay their bills and maintain their current lifestyle. They have also done their Social Security homework and have determined that, between the two of them, they will receive $4,200 per month in benefits. They also receive $350 per month in rent from a tenant who lives in a small carriage house in their backyard. Between their Social Security and the monthly rent income, they will be short $1,450 per month.*

*They do have an additional asset, however. They have been contributing for years to an IRA that has reached a value of $350,000. They realize that they have to figure out how to turn the $350,000 in their IRA into $1,450 per month for the rest of their life. At first glance, it may seem like they will have plenty of money. With some quick calculations, they find they have 240 months, or nearly 20 years, of monthly income* *before they exhaust the account. When you consider income tax, the potential for higher taxes in the future, and market fluctuations (because many IRAs are invested in the market), the amount in the IRA seems to have a little less clout. Every dollar Peter and Nikki take out of the IRA is subject to income tax, and if they leave the remainder in the IRA, they run the risk of losing money in a volatile market. Once they retire and stop getting a paycheck every two weeks, they also stop contributing to their IRA. And when they aren't supplementing its growth with their own money, they are entirely dependent on market growth. That's a scary prospect. They could also withdraw the money from the IRA and put it in a savings account or CD, but removing all the money at once will put them in a tax bracket that will claim a huge portion of the value of the IRA. A seemingly straightforward asset has now become a complicated equation. Peter and Nikki didn't know what to do, so they met with their financial professional.*

*Their financial professional suggested that they use the money to purchase an indexed annuity with an income rider. They selected an annuity that was designed for their specific situation. They took the lump sum from their IRA, placed it in an indexed annuity taking advantage of annual reset so they never lost the value of their investment. In return, they were guaranteed the $1,450 of income per month that they needed to meet their retirement goals. The simplicity of the contract allowed them to do an analysis with their professional just once to understand the product. They basically put their money in an investment crockpot where they didn't have to look at it or manage it. They just needed to let it simmer. In fact, their professional was able to find an annuity for them that allowed them their $1,450 monthly payment with a lump sum of $249,455, leaving them more than $100,000 to reinvest somewhere else. Keep in mind that annuities are* *tax deferred, meaning you will pay tax on the income you receive from an annuity in the year you receive it.*

*By implementing this recommendation, Peter and Nikki accomplish two important parts of their retirement plan:*

1. *They now have a plan in place to provide guaranteed income they cannot out live even if one or both of them live to be over 100 years old.*

2. *Now that their income needs are taken care of, they are able to safely take some risk with the rest of their portfolio.*

## THE SKINNY ON SURRENDER CHARGES

In order to encourage investors to leave their money in their annuity contracts, insurance companies create surrender periods that protect their investments. If you remove your money from the annuity contract during the surrender period, you will pay a penalty and will not be able to receive your entire investment amount back. A typical surrender period is 10 years. If after three years you decide that you want your $100,000 back, the insurance company has that money tied up in bonds and other investments with the understanding that they will have it for another seven years. Because they will take a hit on removing the money from their investments prematurely, you will have to pay a surrender charge that makes up for their loss. During the surrender period, an annuity is not a demand deposit account like a savings or checking account. The higher returns that you are guaranteed from an annuity are dependent on the timeframe you selected. The longer an insurance company can hold your money, the easier it is for them to guarantee a predictable return on it.

If you leave your money in the annuity contract, you get a reliable monthly income no matter what happens in the market. Once the surrender period has expired, you can remove your money whenever you want. Your money becomes liquid again because the insurance company has used it in an investment that fit the timeline of your surrender period. For many people, this is an attractive trade off that can provide a creative solution for filling their income gap.

When is an annuity with an income rider right for you? A good financial professional can help you make that determination by taking the time to listen closely to your situation and understanding what your needs are as you enter retirement. Every salesperson has a bag full of brochures and PowerPoint presentations, but they need to know exactly what the financial concerns of their individual clients are in order to help them make the most informed and beneficial decision. Some people need income today, others need it in five or 10 years. Others may have their income needs met but are planning to move closer to their children and will need to buy a house in 10 years. Or, if you want income in 15 years, you might want to choose a different investment product for 10 years, and then switch to an annuity with an income rider during the last five years of your timeline. Everyone's situation is different and everyone's needs are different. People who are interested in annuities, however, usually need to make decisions that affect their income needs, whether it is filling their income gap, or providing for income down the road.

What happens if you place on a shorter timeframe those assets from which you need to draw an income? Something called single premium immediate annuities may be for you:

## SINGLE PREMIUM IMMEDIATE ANNUITIES (SPIA)

A single premium immediate annuity is simply a contract between you and an insurance company. SPIAs are structured so that you pay a lump sum of money (a single premium) to an insurance company, and they give you a guaranteed income over an agreed upon time period. That time period could be five years, or it could be for the remainder of your lifetime. Guarantees from insurance companies are based on the claims-paying ability of the issuing insurance company.

SPIAs provide investors with a stream of reliable income when they can't afford to take the risk of losing money in a fluctuating market. While there is general faith that the market always trends up, at least in the long-term, if you are focusing on income over a shorter period of time, you may not be able to take a big hit in the market. Beyond normal market volatility, interest rates also come with an inherent level of uncertainty, making it hard to create a dependable income on your own. SPIAs reduce risk for you by giving you regular monthly, quarterly or yearly payments that can begin the moment you buy the contract. Your financial professional can walk you through a series of different payment options to help you select the one that most closely fits your needs.

**Additional Annuity Information:**
- Some contracts will allow you to draw income from the high water mark that the market reaches each year. The income rider will then begin calculating its value from the high water mark.
- Variable annuities, however, can lose money with market fluctuations. As their name suggests, they vary with the market. These annuities do not take advantage of annual reset when the market goes down. The income rider will stay the same, but the value of your actual contract may fall. If you surrender the annuity, the insurance company will pay you the market value of the asset, regardless of whether it matches, exceeds or falls short of the value at which you bought the contract. If its value has dropped significantly, you may be better off taking the income rider without surrendering your contract.
- Income annuities are investment tools that look and feel a bit like Social Security. Every year you allow the money

to grow with the market, and it will "roll up" by a specific amount, paying out a specific percent to you as income each year.

- Annuities can work very well to create income, and a financial professional can help you find the one that best matches your income need, and can also structure it to work perfectly for you.

**Managing Risk Within Your Annuity:**
Just like any investment strategy, the amount of risk needs to fit the comfort level of the investor. Annuities are no exception. Without going into too much detail, here are some additional ways to manage risk with annuity options:

- If you want to structure an annuity investment for growth over a long period of time, you can select a variable annuity. The value of your principal investment follows the market and can lose or gain value with the market. This type of annuity can also have an income rider, but it is really more useful as an accumulation tool that bets on an improving market. A 40-year-old couple, for example, will probably want to structure more for growth and take on more risk than someone in their 70s. The 40-year-old couple may select a variable annuity with an income rider that kicks in when they plan to retire. If it rises with the market or outperforms it, the value of their investment has grown. If the market loses ground over the duration of the contract or their annuity underperforms, they can still rely on the income rider.
- If you are 68 years old and you have more immediate income needs that you need to come up with above and beyond your Social Security, you need a low risk, reliable source of income. If you choose an annuity option, you are looking for something that will pay out an income

right away over a relatively short timeframe. You probably want to opt for a SPIA that pays you immediately and spans a five year period, as well as an additional annuity that begins paying you in five years, and another longer term annuity that begins paying you in 10 years. Bear in mind that each annuity contract has its own costs and fees. Review these with your financial professional before you determine the best products and strategies for your situation.

## CREATING AN INCOME PLAN

Creating an income plan before you retire allows you to satisfy your need for lifetime income and ensures that your lifestyle can last as long as you do. You also want to create a plan that operates in the most efficient way possible. Doing so will give more security to your Need Later Money and will potentially allow you to build your legacy down the road.

In some situations, it might be necessary to employ more than one income vehicle. These strategies, sometimes known as laddering, can be very helpful to retirees with a large income gap or multiple income gaps. Consider the following story:

» *Sophia is 60 years old and is wondering how she can use her assets to provide her with a retirement income. She has a $5,000 per month income need. If she starts withdrawing her Social Security benefit in six years at age 66, it will provide her with $2,200 per month. She also has a pension that kicks in at age 70 that will give her another $1,320 per month.*

*That leaves an income gap of $2,800 from ages 66 to 69, and then an income gap of $1,480 at age 70 and beyond. If Sophia uses only Green Money to solve her income need, she will need to deposit $918,360 at 2 percent interest to meet her monthly goal for her lifetime. If she opts to use Red Money* *and withdraws the amount she needs each month from the market, let's say the S & P 500, she will run out of cash in 10 years if she invested between the years of 2000 and 2012. Suffering a market downturn like that during the period for which she is relying on it for retirement income will change her life, and not for the better.*

*Working with a financial professional to find a better way, Sophia found that she could take a hybrid approach to fill her income gap. Her professional recommended two different income vehicles: one that allowed her to deposit just $190,161 with a 2 percent return, and one that was a $146,000 income annuity. These tools filled her income gap with $336,161, requiring her to spend $582,000 less money to accomplish her goal! Working with a professional to find the right tools for her retirement needs saved Sophia over half a million dollars.*

Here is a basic roadmap of what we have covered so far:

- Review your income needs and look specifically at the shortfall you may have during each year of your retirement based on your Social Security income, and income from any other assets you have.
- Ask yourself where you are in your distribution phase. Is retirement one year away? 10 years away? Last year?
- Determine how much money you need and how you need to structure your existing assets to provide for that need.
- If you have an asset from which you need to generate income, consider options offered by purchasing an income rider on an annuity.

## CHAPTER 5 RECAP //

- Today's income annuities offer retirees an investment that can produce a guaranteed stream of income that functions in a similar way to your Social Security benefit. Income annuities offer guaranteed principal with guaranteed income and are considered a Green Money investment.

- Although an annuity is an income-producing asset that does not subject your income to market risk, it still has the opportunity to grow. Indexed income annuities participate in linked market growth without market loss through a strategy known as indexing. Indexing combined with the power of annual reset gives you both growth and the guaranteed safety of your principal.

- The benefits of an indexed annuity include guarantee of principal, a minimum guaranteed cash value, access to your money, tax deferral, and a guaranteed lifetime income.

- Be sure you understand the features, benefits, costs and fees associated with any annuity product before you invest.

# 6

# WHEN TO PASS
# AND WHEN TO HOLD
# YOUR LINE

*"Speed has never killed anyone.*
*Suddenly becoming stationary… that's what gets you."*
– Jeremy Clarkson

Winning on a racetrack is about learning the course and fine-tuning your vehicle for the track that you're on. During retirement, you're going through major changes that should affect your driving decisions. These changes include the kind of vehicle you are in and the track that you're driving on. There's a great deal of difference between racing strategy when on a Nascar track versus a 1,000-mile off-road trek through the desert. We've spent a good deal of time discussing investment vehicles and the importance of choosing the right vehicles for this unique time in your life. This chapter explains why, during retirement, the track is also different. It has to do with time and events that are outside of your control, and something known in the investing world as the sequence of returns.

## ACCUMULATION DURING YOUR EMPLOYED YEARS

Understanding your Social Security benefit, filling the income gap and making an overall plan that meets your retirement income needs is no small task. Once you have worked with a financial professional to structure your income needs, it's time to take a look at the future. With your immediate income needs met, you have the opportunity to take your additional assets and leverage them for profit to supplement your income in the future, to prepare for anticipated health care costs or to contribute to your legacy. Stable income also means that you should have the staying power to stick with your investment portfolio through the ups and downs in the market.

Your accumulation and growth strategy during retirement deserves different treatment than the growth and accumulation strategy you used when you were employed. Now that you are unemployed, you no longer have a fresh supply of deposits going into your investment accounts. You also have a more restricted time frame. Remember, the stock market is cyclical. It will go up and it will go down. The thing is, *when* it goes up or down is of much greater importance to you as a retiree.

The graph below illustrates the track record of your average investors during their working years. Assuming an initial balance of $100,000 and a 25-year time period, take a look at how the order of the loss affects the balance of two different portfolios. *The order of losses and gains is what's known as the sequence of returns.* We will assume an equal account balance and an annual income of zero dollars, because both investors are working and not taking any money out of their savings accounts. Because they are employed, they don't need the extra income, so the money is left alone to grow. This is why the typical buy-and-hold accumulation strategies employed during your working years are so effective: you aren't taking money out, you consistently put money in, and you have time to recover from any loss. Take a look at the numbers below and see for yourself.

**SEQUENCE OF RETURNS DURING YOUR EMPLOYED YEARS:**

| Age | Annual Return | Portfolio A Year End Balance | Annual Return | Portfolio B Year End Balance |
|---|---|---|---|---|
| 45 | | 100,000 | | 100,000 |
| 46 | 32% | 131,690 | -37% | 63,000 |
| 47 | -3% | 127,594 | 5% | 66,459 |
| 48 | 30% | 166,472 | 16% | 76,986 |
| 49 | 8% | 179,158 | 5% | 80,766 |
| 50 | 10% | 197,217 | 11% | 89,553 |
| 51 | 1% | 199,820 | 29% | 115,237 |
| 52 | 38% | 274,912 | -22% | 89,770 |
| 53 | 23% | 338,032 | -12% | 79,105 |
| 54 | 33% | 450,800 | -9% | 71,898 |
| 55 | 29% | 579,638 | 21% | 87,026 |
| 56 | 21% | 701,594 | 29% | 111,898 |
| 57 | -9% | 637,679 | 33% | 149,227 |
| 58 | -12% | 561,923 | 23% | 183,490 |
| 59 | -22% | 437,738 | 38% | 252,445 |
| 60 | 29% | 563,281 | 1% | 255,777 |
| 61 | 11% | 624,566 | 10% | 281,560 |
| 62 | 5% | 655,232 | 8% | 303,014 |
| 63 | 16% | 759,021 | 30% | 395,343 |
| 64 | 5% | 800,691 | -3% | 383,048 |
| 65 | -37% | 504,436 | 32% | 504,436 |

Notice that at the end of the 25 years, the portfolio balance of the two investors is exactly the same, even though Investor B sustained a 37-percent loss in the first year while Investor B enjoyed a 32-percent return. The beginning and ending balance of both portfolios are the same, and the returns were also the same. The difference was the order in which those returns were calculated. If you averaged 8.43 percent return over 20 years, does the sequence of the gains and losses matter? During your working years, no, it does not.

Now let's compare that with accumulation during retirement.

## UNDERSTANDING THE SEQUENCE OF RETURNS DURING RETIREMENT

Trying to time the market during retirement might be compared to knowing when to pass and when to hold the line when racing. Making a mistake during retirement could very well take you out of the race for good, however. During retirement, loss is even worse than most people realize. The diagram below shows you how the sequence of returns can work against you during your unemployed years in a way that didn't matter when you working and saving.

The graph below shows portfolios A and B. We will assume an equal account balance of $504,436, using the end balance of our imaginary investors who, at the age of 65, have now retired. They are both taking out the same amount of income—5 percent of the principal beginning in the first year, and increasing by 3 percent each year to compensate for inflation. This example also covers a 20-year time span in the life of the investors from ages 65 to 85. Also note that no more money is going into the savings accounts.

Now draw your eyes down the graph and look at what happens to the investor in portfolio B at the age of 84. He runs out of money, and his retirement effectively goes into a crash and burn. Compare that with investor A: at the age of 84, he has an account balance of over $2 million dollars. What did he do so differently? Was he a superior driver? Did he have inside information about the track? Did have a faster car? Nope. It was nothing at all that he did or didn't do. In fact, the success of his returns had nothing at all to do with him and everything to do with the track that he was on. The difference was the order of the returns. Now ask yourself, do you want the safety of your retirement dependent on factors completely outside of your control?

**SEQUENCE OF RETURNS DURING UNEMPLOYMENT**

| Age | Annual Return | Portfolio A Year End Balance | Annual Return | Portfolio B Year End Balance |
|-----|-----|-----|-----|-----|
| 65 | | **504,436** | | **504,436** |
| 66 | 32% | 633,450 | -37% | 290,000 |
| 67 | -3% | 588,000 | 5% | 280,171 |
| 68 | 30% | 740,641 | 16% | 298,028 |
| 69 | 8% | 769,759 | 5% | 285,343 |
| 70 | 10% | 819,213 | 11% | 288,250 |
| 71 | 1% | 801,045 | 29% | 341,938 |
| 72 | 38% | 1,072,227 | -22% | 236,519 |
| 73 | 23% | 1,287,663 | -12% | 177,673 |
| 74 | 33% | 1,685,558 | -9% | 129,818 |
| 75 | 29% | 2,134,671 | 21% | 124,513 |
| 76 | 21% | 2,550,208 | 29% | 126,500 |
| 77 | -9% | 2,283,278 | 33% | 134,095 |
| 78 | -12% | 1,976,381 | 23% | 129,239 |
| 79 | -22% | 1,502,887 | 38% | 141,094 |
| 80 | 29% | 1,896,101 | 1% | 105,142 |
| 81 | 11% | 2,063,447 | 10% | 76,791 |
| 82 | 5% | 2,124,645 | 8% | 42,524 |
| 83 | 16% | 2,419,867 | 30% | 14,160 |
| 84 | 5% | 2,510,157 | -3% | 0 |
| 85 | -37% | **1,537,562** | 32% | **0** |

Whether the market is high or low on the day you retire and during the years just after your retirement is out of your control, yet it can have a big impact on the smoothness of your retirement years. Most people don't realize that it's the *sequence of returns* that influences the value of their account even more than the actual rate of return. A 65-year-old male retiring today has a 40 percent chance of living to age 85, and a female has more than a 50 percent chance of living to 85.* That puts a real test on the ability of your savings to last as long as you do.

*We never want you to run out of money before you run out of life.* As we have seen throughout this book, investing in traditional ways such as pulling out 6 percent withdrawals from market investments leads to potential disaster. Investors are facing unique and challenging times. Safe money investments such as bank CDs are paying interest rates too low to keep up with inflation, while market anomalies and rising global tensions directly affect the stability of income in market investments. This fear and uncertainty naturally facilitates the need for another investment vehicle. There are ways to guarantee income and grow your money during retirement that don't put the stability of your future at risk. Ask your financial professional what accumulation strategies might be right for you during retirement.

## CHAPTER 7 RECAP //

- The timing of market downturns is more critical to retirees than to the average investor. During the accumulation years, the sequence of returns does not matter as much as it does during the distribution years. If you are making withdrawals on a market investment without first protecting your income, and the account suffers a loss, rapid depletion of your funds will change what the future of your retirement looks like.

---

* *https://www.soa.org/files/research/projects/research-key-finding-longevity.pdf*

# 7

# JUMPING OUT OF A PLANE WITHOUT A PARACHUTE

*"You don't need a parachute to skydive, you only
need a parachute to skydive twice."*
– Simon Drew

It can be challenging to watch the stock market's erratic changes every month, week or even every day. When you have your money riding on it, the ride can feel like a freefall during which you realize you forgot to pack a parachute. When you are managing your money by yourself, emotions like fear and panic inevitably enter into the mix. The Dow Jones Industrial Average and the S&P 500 represent more to you than market fluctuations. They represent a portion of your retirement. It's hard not to be emotional about it.

Everyone knows you should buy low and sell high. But this is what is more likely to happen:

The market takes a downturn, similar to the 2008 crash, and investors see as much as a 37 percent loss in their stock holdings*. It's hard to watch, and it's harder to bear the pain of losing that much money. The math of rebounds means that they will need to rely on even larger gains just to get back to where things were before the downturn. They sell. But eventually, and inevitably, the market begins to rise again. Maybe slowly, maybe with some moderate growth, but by the time the average investor notices an upward trend and wants to buy in again, they have already missed a great deal of the gains.

> » *Carolyn's situation illustrates how market volatility can have major repercussions for an individual investor. Carolyn works for Acme Paper Company for 34 years. During her time there, she acquires bonuses and pay raises that often include shares of stock in the company. She also dedicates part of her paycheck every month to a 401(k) that bought Acme stock. By the time she retires, Carolyn has $250,000 worth of Acme stock.*
>
> *Although she had contributes to her 401(k) account every month, Carolyn doesn't cultivate any other assets that could generate income for her during retirement. Carolyn also retires early at age 62 because of her failing health. The commute to work every day was becoming difficult in her weakened condition and she wanted to enjoy the rest of her life in retirement instead of working at Acme.*
>
> *Because she retires early, Carolyn fails to maximize her Social Security benefit. While she lives a modest lifestyle, her income needs will still be $3,500 per month. Carolyn's*

---

\* *http://www.investopedia.com/articles/economics/09/subprime-market-2008.asp*

*monthly Social Security check will only cover $1,900, leaving her with a $1,600 income shortfall. To supplement her Social Security check, Carolyn sells $1,600 of her Acme stock each month to meet her income needs. A $250,000 401(k) is nothing to sneeze at, but reducing its value by $1,600 every month will barely last Carolyn 10 years. And that's if the market stays neutral or grows modestly. If the market takes a downturn, the money that Carolyn relied on to fill her income shortfall will rapidly diminish. Even if the market starts going up in a couple of years, it will take much larger gains for her to recover the value that she lost.*

*Unhappily for Carolyn, she retired in 2007, just before the major market downturn that lasted for several years. She lost more than 20 percent of the value of her stock. Because Carolyn needed to sell her stock to meet her basic income needs, the market price of the stock was secondary to her need for the money. When she needed money, she was forced to sell however many shares she needed to fill her income shortfall that month. And if she has a financial crisis, involving her need for medical care, for example, she will be forced to sell stock even if the market is low and her shares are nearly worthless.*

*Carolyn realizes that she could have relied on an investment structured to deliver her a regular income while protecting the value of her investment. She could have kept her $250,000 from diminishing while enjoying her lifestyle into retirement regardless of the volatility of the market. Ideally, Carolyn would have restructured her 401(k) to reflect the level of risk that she was able to take. In her case, she would have had most of her money in Green Money assets, allowing her to rely on the value of her assets when she needed them.*

In 2013, DALBAR, the well-respected financial services market research firm, released their annual "Quantitative Analysis of Investment Behavior" report (QAIB). The report studied the impact of market volatility on individual investors: people like Carolyn, or anyone who was managing (or mismanaging) their own investments in the stock market.

## ARE YOU JUMPING WITHOUT A CHUTE?
### *THE RESULTS OF THE DALBAR STUDY*
According to the study, volatility not only caused investors to make decisions based on their emotions, those decisions also harmed their investments and prevented them from realizing potential gains. So why do people meddle so much with their investments when the market is fluctuating? Part of the reason is that many people have financial obligations that they don't have control over. Significant expenses like house payments, the unexpected cost of replacing a broken-down car, and medical bills can put people in a position where they need money.

**If they need to sell investments to come up with that money, they don't have the luxury of selling when they *want* to. They must sell when they *need* to.**

DALBAR's "Quantitative Analysis of Investor Behavior" has been used to measure the effects of investors' buying, selling and mutual fund switching decisions since 1994. The QAIB shows time and time again over nearly a 20 year period that the average investor earns less, and in many cases, significantly less than the performance of mutual funds suggests. QAIB's goal is to improve independent investor performance and to help financial professionals provide helpful advice and investment strategies that address the concerns and behaviors of the average investor.

An excerpt from the report claims that:*

---

*2013 QAIB, Dalbar, March 2013

*"QAIB offers guidance on how and where investor behaviors can be improved. No matter what the state of the mutual fund industry, boom or bust: Investment results are more dependent on investor behavior than on fund performance. Mutual fund investors who hold on to their investments are more successful than those who time the market.*

*QAIB uses data from the Investment Company Institute (ICI), Standard & Poor's and Barclays Capital Index Products to compare mutual fund investor returns to an appropriate set of benchmarks.*

*There are actually three primary causes for the chronic shortfall for both equity and fixed income investors:*

1. *Capital not available to invest. This accounts for 25 percent to 35 percent of the shortfall.*
2. *Capital needed for other purposes. This accounts for 35 percent to 45 percent of the shortfall.*
3. *Psychological factors. These account for 45 percent to 55 percent of the shortfall."*

**The key findings of Dalbar's QAIB report provide compelling statistics about how individual investment strategies produced negative outcomes for the majority of investors:**

- Psychological factors account for 45 percent to 55 percent of the chronic investment return shortfall for both equity and fixed income investors.
- Asset allocation is designed to handle the investment decision-making for the investor, which can materially reduce the shortfall due to psychological factors.
- Successful asset allocation investing requires investors to act on two critical imperatives:
  1. Balance capital preservation and appreciation so that they are aligned with the investor's objective.
  2. Select a qualified allocator.

- The best way for an investor to determine their risk tolerance is to utilize a risk tolerance assessment. However, these assessments must be accessible and usable.

- Evaluating allocator quality requires analysis of the allocator's underlying investments, decision making process and whether or not past efforts have produced successful outcomes.

- Choosing a top allocator makes a significant difference in the investment results one will achieve.

- Mutual fund retention rates suggest that the average investor has not remained invested for long enough periods to derive the potential benefits of the investment markets.

- Retention rates for asset allocation funds exceed those of equity and fixed income funds by over a year.

- Investors' ability to correctly time the market is highly dependent on the direction of the market. Investors generally guess right more often in up markets. However, in 2012 investors guessed right only 42 percent of the time during a bull market.

- Analysis of investor fund flows compared to market performance further supports the argument that investors are unsuccessful at timing the market. Market upswings rarely coincide with mutual fund inflows while market downturns do not coincide with mutual fund outflows.

- Average equity mutual fund investors gained 15.56 percent compared to a gain of 15.98 percent that just holding the S&P 500 produced.

- The shortfall in the long-term annualized return of the average mutual fund equity investor and the S&P 500 continued to decrease in 2012.

- The fixed-income investor experienced a return of 4.68 percent compared to an advance of 4.21 percent on the Barclays Aggregate Bond Index.

- The average fixed income investor has failed to keep up with inflation in nine out of the last 14 years.*

It doesn't take a financial services market research report to tell you that market volatility is out of your control. The report does prove, however, that before you experience market volatility, you should have an investment plan, and when the market is fluctuating, you should stand by your investment plan. You should also review and discuss your investment plan with your financial professional on a regular basis, ensuring he/she is aware of any changes in your goals, financial circumstances, your health or your risk tolerance. When the economy is under stress and the markets are volatile, investors can feel vulnerable. That vulnerability causes people to tinker with their portfolios in an attempt to outsmart the market. Financial professionals, however, don't try to time the market for their clients. They try to tap into the gains that can be realized by committing to long-term investment strategies.

**CHAPTER 7 RECAP //**

- When you are relying on your investments to provide you with income, you risk taking a double hit—one from the withdrawal and then again from any market downturns.
- Emotions inevitably enter the mix during stock market downturns. According to the DALBAR "Quantitative Analysis of Investment Behavior" report released in 2013, the average fixed income investor managing their money alone failed to keep up with inflation in nine out of the last 14 years.

---

*2013 QAIB, Dalbar, March 2013*

# 8

## MAKING THE
## TANDEM SKYDIVE:
## YELLOW MONEY

*"Any idiot can fly a plane, but it takes a special
kind of idiot to jump out of one."*
– Author Unknown

Now that you've calculated the Rule of 100, determined how
much risk you have and how much you want, and you've determined how much Green Money you need to meet your short-
term and mid-term income needs, it's time to look at what you
have left. The money you have left after you've calculated your
Green Money needs has the potential of becoming Red Money:
your stocks, mutual funds and other investment products that
you want to continue accumulating value with the market. You

now have the luxury of taking a closer second look at your Red Money to determine how you would like to manage it.

As you read earlier in the key findings of the DALBAR report, the deck is stacked against the individual investor. Remember that the average investor on a fixed income failed to keep pace with inflation in nine of the last 14 years, meaning the inherent risk in managing your Red Money is very real and could have a plummeting impact on your assets. So, how much of your Red Money do you invest, and in what kinds of markets, investment products and stocks do you invest? There are a lot of different directions in which you can take your Red Money. One thing is for sure: significant accumulation depends on investing in the market. How you go about doing it is different for everyone. Gathering stocks, bonds and investment funds together in a portfolio without a cohesive strategy behind them could cause you to miss out on the benefits of a more thoughtful and planful approach. The end result is that you may never really understand what your money is doing, where and how it is really invested, and which investment principles are behind the investment products you hold. While you may have goals for each individual piece of your portfolio, it is likely that you don't have a comprehensive plan for your Red Money, which may mean that *you are taking on more risk than you would like, and are getting less return for it than is possible.*

Enter **Yellow Money.** Yellow Money is money that is managed by a professional *with a purpose.* After your income needs are met and you have assets that you would like to dedicate to accumulation, there are decisions you need to make about how to invest those assets. You can buy stocks, index funds, mutual funds, bonds—you name it—you can invest in it. However, the difference between Red Money and Yellow Money is that Yellow Money has a cohesive strategy behind it that is *implemented by a professional.* When you manage your Red Money with an investment plan, it becomes Yellow Money: *money that is being managed* *with a specific purpose, a specific set of focused goals and a specific strategy in mind.* Yellow Money is still a type of Red Money. It comes with different levels of risk. But Yellow Money is under the watchful eye of professionals who have a stake in the success of your money in the market and who can recommend a range of strategies from those designed for preservation to those targeting rapid growth. You don't want to miss out on achieving the right level of risk, and more importantly, composing a careful plan for the return of your assets.

It can be helpful to think of Red Money and Yellow Money with this analogy:

If you always wanted to skydive but didn't have the time and resources to invest in weeks of lessons, you might hire a tandem instructor to make the jump with you. During a tandem skydive, a student skydiver is attached to a certified tandem instructor by a harness. As the student, you are given the necessary gear, but when it comes time to jump out of the plan, you are not alone. You are attached to your instructor, and together you exit the plane, descend in freefall, and pilot a single canopy to the ground. For most people who want to experience the thrill of skydiving, a tandem skydive is the method to choose. A good instructor knows when to jump, when to deploy the chute and how to land without getting hurt.

Red Money is like jumping out of an airplane all by yourself, with no training or instruction. Yellow Money is like working with a tandem instructor. With Yellow Money, you are still jumping out of a plane, but now you have a professional who is working with you and free falling with you, so they have a personal stake in your success.

## TAKING A CLOSER LOOK AT YOUR PORTFOLIO

Think about your investment portfolio. Think specifically of what you would consider your Red Money. Do you know what is there? You may have several different investment products like individual mutual funds, bond accounts, stocks, etc. You may have inherited a stock portfolio from a relative, or you might be invested in a bond account offered by the company for which you worked due to your familiarity with them. While you may or may not be managing your investments individually, the reality is that you probably don't have an overall management strategy for all of your investments. Investments that aren't managed are simply Red Money, or money that is at risk in the market.

Harnessing the earning potential of your Red Money relies on more than a collection of stocks and bonds, however. It needs guided management. A good Yellow Money manager uses the knowledge they have about the level of risk with which you are comfortable, what you need or want to use your money for, when you want or need it and how you want to use it. The Yellow Money objects that they choose for you will still have a certain level of risk, but under the right management, control and process, you have a far better chance of a successful outcome that meets your specific needs.

When you sit down with an investment professional, you can look at all of your assets together. Chances are that you have accumulated a number of different assets over the last 20, 30 or 50 years. You may have a 401(k), an IRA, a Roth IRA, an account of self-directed stocks, a brokerage account, etc. Wherever you put your money, a financial professional will go through your assets and help you determine the level of risk to which you are exposed now and should be exposed in the future.

Here is a typical example of how an investment professional can be helpful to a future retiree with Yellow Money needs:

> » *Stephanie is 65 years old and wants to retire in two years. She has a 401(k) from her job to which she has contributed for 26 years. She also has some stocks that her late husband*

*managed. Stephanie also has $55,000 in a mutual fund that her sister recommended to her five years ago and $30,000 in another mutual fund that she heard about at work. She takes a look at her assets one day and decides that she doesn't understand what they add up to or what kind of retirement they will provide. She decides to meet with an investment professional. Stephanie's professional immediately asks her:*

*1. Does she know exactly where all of her money is?* *Stephanie doesn't know much about all her husband's stocks, which have now become hers. Their value is at $100,000 invested in three large cap companies. Stephanie is unsure of the companies and whether she should hold or sell them.*

*2. Does she know what types of assets she owns?* *Yes and no. She knows she had a 401(k) and IRAs, but she is unfamiliar with her husband's self-directed stock portfolio or the type of mutual funds she owns. Furthermore she is unclear as to how to manage the holdings as she nears retirement.*

*3. Does she know the strategies behind each one of the investment products she owns?* *While Stephanie knows she had a 401(k), an IRA and mutual fund holdings, she doesn't know how her 401(k) is organized or how to make it more conservative as she nears retirement. She is unsure whether her IRA is a Roth or traditional variety and how to draw income from them? She really does not have specific investment principles guiding her investment decisions, and she doesn't know anything about her husband's individual stocks. One major concern for Stephanie is whether her family would be okay if she were not around?*

*After determining Stephanie's assets, her financial professional prepares a consolidated report that lays out all of her assets for her to review. Her professional explains each one of them to her. Stephanie discovers that although she is two years away from retiring, her 401(k) is organized with an amount of risk with which she is not comfortable. Sixty percent of her 401(k) is at risk, far off the mark if we abide by the Rule of 100. Stephanie opts to be more conservative than the Rule of 100 suggests, as she will rely on her 401(k) for most of her immediate income needs after retirement. Stephanie's professional also points out several instances of overlap between her mutual funds. Stephanie learns that while she is comfortable with one of her mutual funds, she does not agree with the management principles of the other. In the end, Stephanie's professional helps her re-organize her 401(k) to secure her more Green Money for retirement income. Her professional also uses her mutual fund and her husband's stock assets to create a growth oriented investment plan that Stephanie will rely on for Need Later Money in 15 years when she plans on relocating closer to her children and grandchildren. By creating an overall investment strategy, Stephanie is able to meet her targeted goals in retirement. Stephanie's financial professional worked closely with her and her tax professional to minimize the tax impact of any asset sales on Stephanie's situation.*

Like Stephanie, you may have several savings vehicles: a 401(k), an IRA to which you regularly contribute, some mutual funds to which you make monthly contributions, etc. But what is your *overall investment strategy?* Do you have one in place? Do you want one that will help you meet your retirement goals? Yellow Money looks at *ALL* your accounts and all their different strategies to create a plan that helps them all work together. Your current investment situation may not reflect your wishes. As a matter of fact, it likely doesn't.

You may have a better understanding of your assets than Stephanie did, but even someone with an investment strategy can benefit from having a financial professional review their portfolio:

» *Randy is 69 years old. He retired four years ago. He relied on income from an IRA for three years in order to increase his Social Security benefit. He also made significant investments in 36 different mutual funds. He chose to diversify among the funds by selecting a portion for growth, another for good dividends, another that focused on promising small cap companies and a final portion that work like index funds. All the money that Randy had in mutual funds he considered Need Later Money that he wanted to rely on in his 80s. After the stock market took a hit in 2008, Randy lost some confidence in his investments and decided to sit down with a financial professional to see if his portfolio was able to recover.*

*The professional Randy met with was able to determine what goals he had in mind. Specifically, the financial professional determined what Randy actually wanted and needed the money for, and when he needed it. His professional also looked inside each of the mutual funds and discovered several instances of overlap. While Randy had created diversity in his portfolio by selecting funds focused on different goals, he didn't account for overlap in the companies in which the funds were invested. Out of the 36 funds, his professional found that 20 owned nearly identical stock. While most of the companies were good investments, the high instance of overlap did not contribute to the healthy investment diversity that Randy wanted. Randy's financial professional also provided him with a report that explained the concentration ratio of his holdings (noting how much of his portfolio was contained within the top 25 stock holdings), the percentage of his portfolio that each company in which he invested in represented (showing the percentage of net assets that each company made up as an overall position in his portfolio) and the portfolio date of his account (showing when the funds in his portfolio were last updated: as funds are required to report updates only twice per year, it was possible that some of his fund reports could be six months old).*

*Randy's professional consolidated his assets into one investment management strategy. This allowed Randy's investments to be managed by someone he trusted who knew his specific investment goals and needs. Eliminating redundancy and overlap in his portfolio was easy to do but difficult to detect since Randy had multiple funds with multiple brokerage firms. Randy sat down with a professional to see if his mutual funds could perform well, and he left with a consolidated management plan and a money manager that understood him personally. That's Yellow Money at its best.*

## AVOIDING EMOTIONAL INVESTING

There's no way around it; people get emotional about their money. And for good reason. You've spent your life working for it, exchanging your time and talent for it, and making decisions about how to invest it, save it and make it grow. The maintenance of your lifestyle and your plans for retirement all depend on it. The best investment strategies, however, don't rely on emotions. One of Yellow Money's greatest strengths lies in the fact that it is managed by someone who understands your needs and desires, but doesn't make decisions about your money under the influence of emotion.

A well-managed investment account meets your goals as a whole, not in individualized and piecemeal ways. Professional money managers do this by creating requirements for each type of investment in which they put your money. We'll call them "screens." Your money manager will run your holdings through the screens they have created to evaluate different types of investment strategies. A professionally managed account will only have holdings that meet the requirements laid out in the overall management plan that was designed to meet your investment goals. The holdings that don't make it through the screens, the ones that don't contribute to your investment goals, are sold and redistributed to investments that your financial professional has determined to be appropriate.

Different screens apply to different Yellow Money strategies. For example, if one of your goals is significant growth, which would require taking on more risk alongside the potential for more return, an investment professional would screen for companies that have high rates of revenue and sales growth, high earnings growth, rising profit margins, and innovative products. On the other hand, if you want your portfolio to be used for income, which would call for lower risk and less return, your professional would screen for dividend yield and sector diversification. *Every investor has a different goal, and every goal requires a customized strategy that uses quantitative screens.* A professional will create a portfolio that reflects your investment desires. If some of the current assets you own complement the strategies that your professional recommends, those will likely stay in your portfolio.

Screening your assets removes emotions from the equation. It removes attachment to underperforming or overly risky investments. Financial professionals aren't married to particular stocks or mutual funds for any reason. They go by the numbers and see your portfolio through a lens shaped by your retirement goals. Your professional understands your wants and needs, and creates an investment strategy that takes your life events and future plans into account. It's a planful approach, and it allows you to tap into the tools and resources of a professional who has built a career around successful investing. Managing money is a full-time job and is best left to a professional money manager.

Removing emotions from investing also allows you to be unaffected by the day-to-day volatility of the market. Your financial professional doesn't ask where the market is going to be in a year, three years or a month from now. If you look at the value of the stock market from the beginning of the twentieth century to today, it's going up. Despite the Great Depression, despite the 1987 crash, despite the 2008 market downturn, the market, as a whole, trends up. Remember the major market downturn in 2008 when the market lost 37 percent of its value*? Not only did it completely recover, it has far exceeded its 2008 value. Emotional investing led countless people to sell low as the market went down, and buy the same shares back when the market started to recover. That's an expensive way to do business. While you can't afford to lose money that you need in two, three or five years, your Need Later Money has time to grow. The best way to do so is to make it Yellow.

## CREATING AN INVESTMENT STRATEGY

Just like Stephanie and Randy, chances are that you can benefit from taking a more managed investment approach tailored to your goals. Yellow Money is generally Need Later Money that you want to grow for needs you'll have in at least 10 years. You can work with your financial planner to create investments that meet your needs within different timeframes. You may need to rely on some of your Yellow Money in 10, 15 or 20 years, whether for additional income, a large purchase you plan on making or a vacation. Whatever you want it for, you will need it down the road. A financial professional can help you rescale the risk of your assets as they grow, helping you lock in your profits and secure a source of income you can depend on later.

So what does a Yellow Money account look like? Here's what it *doesn't* look like: a portfolio with 49 small cap mutual funds, a dozen individual stocks and an assortment of bond accounts. A brokerage account with a hodgepodge of investments, even if goal-oriented, is not a professionally managed account. It's still

---

* *http://www.investopedia.com/articles/economics/09/subprime-market-2008.asp*

Red Money. Remember, Yellow Money is a managed account that has an overarching investment Philosophy. When you look at making investments that will perform to meet your future income needs, the burning question becomes: How much should you have in the market and how should it be invested? Working with a professional will help you determine how much risk you should take, how to balance your assets so they will meet your goals and how to plan for the big ticket items, like health care expenses, that may be in your future. Yes, Yellow Money is exposed to risk, but by working with a professional, you can manage that risk in a productive way.

## WHY YELLOW MONEY?

If you have met your immediate income needs for retirement, why bother with professionally managing your other assets? The money you have accumulated above and beyond your income needs probably has a greater purpose. It may be for your children or grandchildren. You may want to give money to a charity or organization that you admire. In short, you may want to craft your legacy. It would be advantageous to grow your assets in the best manner possible. A financial professional has built a career around managing money in profitable ways. They are experts under the supervision of the organization that they represent.

Turning to Yellow Money also means that you don't have to burden yourself with the time commitment, the stress, and the cost of determining how to manage your money. Yellow Money can help you better enjoy your retirement. Do you want to sit down in your home office every day and determine how to best allocate your assets, or do you want to be living your life while someone else manages your money for you? When the majority of your Red Money is managed with a specific purpose by a financial professional, you don't have to be worrying about which stocks to buy and sell today or tomorrow.

## SEEKING FINANCIAL ADVICE: STOCK BROKERS VS. INVESTMENT ADVISOR REPRESENTATIVES

Investors basically have access to two types of advice in today's financial world: advice from stock brokers and advice given by investment advisors. Most investors, however, don't know the difference between types of advice and the people from whom they receive advice. Today, there are two primary types of advice offered to investors: advice given by a commission-based registered representative (brokers) and advice given by fee-based Investment Advisor Representatives. Unfortunately, many investors are not aware that a difference exists; nor have they been explained the distinction between the two types of advice. In a survey taken by TD Ameritrade, the top reasons investors choose to work with an independent registered investment advisor are:*

- Registered Investment Advisors are required, as fiduciaries, to offer advice that is in the best interest of clients
- More personalized service and competitive fee structure offered at a Registered Investment Advisor firm
- Dissatisfaction with full commission brokers

The truth is that there is a great deal of difference between stock brokers and investment advisor representatives. For starters, investment advisor representatives are obligated to act in an investor's best interests in all aspects of a financial relationship. Confusion continues to exist among investors struggling to find the best financial advice out there and the most credible sources of advice.

Here is some information to help clear up the confusion so you can find good advice from a professional you can trust:

---

*2011 Advisor Sentiment Study, commissioned by TD AMERITRADE. TD Ameritrade, Inc.*

- Investment advisor representatives have the fiduciary duty to act in a client's best interest at all times with every investment decision they make. Stock brokers and brokerage firms usually do not act as fiduciaries to their investors and are not obligated to make decisions that are entirely in the best interest of their customers. For example, if you decide you want to invest in precious metals, a stock broker would offer you a precious metals account from their firm. An Investment Advisor would find you a precious metals account that is the best fit for you based on the investment strategy of your portfolio.

- Investment advisors give their clients a Form ADV describing the methods that the professional uses to do business. An Investment Advisor also obtains client consent regarding any conflicts of interest that could exist with the business of the professional.

- Stock brokers and brokerage firms are not obligated to provide comparable types of disclosure to their customers.

- Whereas stock brokers and firms routinely earn large profits by trading as principal with customers, Investment Advisors cannot trade with clients as principal (except in very limited and specific circumstances).

- Investment Advisors charge a pre-negotiated fee with their clients in advance of any transactions. They cannot earn additional profits or commissions from their customers' investments without prior consent. Registered Investment Advisors are commonly paid an asset-based fee that aligns their interests with those of their clients. Brokerage firms and stock brokers, on the other hand, have much different payment agreements. Their revenues may increase regardless of the performance of their customers' assets.

- Unlike brokerage firms, where investment banking and underwriting are commonplace, Registered Investment

Advisors must manage money in the best interests of their customers. Because Registered Investment Advisors charge set fees for their services, their focus is on their client. Brokerage firms may focus on other aspects of the firm that do not contribute to the improvement of their clients' assets.

Just to drive home the point, here is what a fiduciary duty to a client means for a Registered Investment Advisor. Registered Investment Advisors must:*

- Always act in the best interest of their client and make investment decisions that reflect their goals.
- Identify and monitor securities that are illiquid.
- When appropriate, employ fair market valuation procedures.
- Observe procedures regarding the allocation of investment opportunities, including new issues and the aggregation of orders.
- Have policies regarding affiliated broker-dealers and maintenance of brokerage accounts.
- Disclose all conflicts of interest.
- Have policies on use of brokerage commissions for research.
- Have policies regarding directed brokerage, including step-out trades and payment for order flow.
- Abide by a code of ethics.

---

* *2011 Advisor Sentiment Study, commissioned by TD AMERITRADE. TD Ameritrade, Inc.*

## CHAPTER 8 RECAP //

- Yellow Money is money that is managed by a professional with a purpose. It is still considered a type of Red Money, but there is a dedicated direction, strategy and end goal in mind, which makes it less dangerous.
- Red Money is like jumping out of an airplane with no instruction, alone, in the dark. You might get lucky and make it to where you want to go but it's a dangerous journey. With Yellow Money, you are still jumping out of an airplane, but now you are paired with a trained professional who is acting in your best interest.
- Yellow Money is managed without emotions. A financial professional qualified to manage money uses a specific criteria designed to fit into your overall financial plan so that it works the way you want it to.

*9*

# NEW WAYS TO LOOK AT YOUR INVESTMENT VEHICLES

*"A chance is what you take before you think about it.*
*A calculated risk is what you take after you have evaluated*
*all possible factors and have determined that risk."*
– Craig Elliot

In Chapter 1, we discussed how today's investment options require advice that is relevant to today. Traditional, outdated investment strategies are not only ineffective, they can be harmful to the average investor. One of the most traditional ways of thinking about investing is the risk versus reward trade-off. It goes something like this.

Investment options that are considered safer carry less risk, but also offer the potential for less return. Riskier investment options carry the burden of volatility and a greater potential for loss, but they also offer a greater potential for large rewards. Most professionals move their clients back and forth along this range, shifting between investments that are safer and investments that are structured for growth. Essentially, the old rules of investing dictate that you can either choose relative safety *or* return, but you can't have both.

Updated investment strategies work with the flexibility of liquidity to remake the rules. Here is how:

There are three dimensions that are inherent in any investment: *Liquidity, Safety,* and *Return.* You can maximize any two of these dimensions at the expense of the third. If you choose Safety and Liquidity, this is like keeping your assets in a checking account or savings account. This option delivers a lot of Safety and Liquidity, but at the expense of any Return. On the other hand, if you choose Liquidity and Return, meaning you have the potential for great return and can still reclaim your money whenever you choose, you will likely be exposed to a very high level of risk.

Understanding Liquidity can help you break the old Risk versus Safety trade-off. By identifying assets from which you don't require Liquidity, you can place yourself in a position to potentially profit from relatively safe investments that provide a higher than average rate of return.

Choosing Safety and Return over Liquidity can have significant impacts on the accumulation of your assets. In Greg's case, the paradigm shift from earning and saving to leveraging assets was a costly one.

» *Greg is a corn and soybean farmer with 1,200 acres of land. He routinely retains somewhere between $40,000 and $80,000 in his checking and savings accounts. If a major* *piece of equipment fails and needs repair or replacement, Greg will need the money available to pay for the equipment and carry on with farming. If the price of feed for his cattle goes up one year, he will need to compensate for the increased overhead to his farming operation. He isn't a particularly wealthy farmer, but he has little choice but to keep a portion of money on hand in case something comes up and he must access it quickly. Most of his capital is held in livestock in the pasture or crops in the ground tied up for six to eight months of the year. When a major financial need arises, Greg can't just harvest 10 acres of soybeans and use them for payment. He needs to depend heavily on Liquidity in order to be a successful farmer.*

*Old habits die hard, however, and when Greg finally hangs up his overalls and quits farming, he keeps his bank accounts flush with cash, just like in the old days. After selling the farm and the equipment, Greg keeps a huge portion of the profits in Liquid investments because that's what he is familiar with. Unfortunately for Greg, with his pile of money sitting in his checking account, he isn't even keeping pace with inflation. After all his hard work as a farmer, his money is losing value every day because he didn't shift to a paradigm of leveraging his assets to generate income and accumulate value.*

*Almost anything would be a better option for Greg than clinging to Liquidity. He could have done something better to get either more return from his money or more safety, and at the very least would not have lost out to inflation.*

As you can see, choosing Liquidity solely can be a costly option. The sooner you want your money back, the less you can leverage it for Safety or Return. If you have the option of putting your money in a long-term investment, you will be sacrificing Liquidity, but potentially gaining both Safety and Return. Rethinking your approach to money in this way can make a world of difference and can provide you with a structured way to generate income while allowing the value of your asset to grow over time. **The question is, how much Liquidity do you *really* need?** Think about it. If you haven't sat down and created an income plan for your retirement, your perceived need for Liquidity is a guess. You don't know how much cash you'll need to fill the income gap if you don't know the amount of your Social Security benefit of the total of your other income options. If you *have* determined your income need and have made a plan for filling your income gap, you can partition your assets based on when you will need them. With an income plan in place, *you can use new rules to enjoy both Safety and Return from your assets.*

## CHAPTER 9 RECAP //

- The three aspects of any investment include liquidity, safety, and return. You can choose to maximize any two against the third.

- Choosing to maximize liquidity alone can be an expensive option because the sooner you need your money back, the less you can leverage it for safety and return. To plan for a successful retirement in today's economy requires a creative use of today's financial tools.

# 10

# YOUR TAX TUNE-UP

*"I'm gonna give you an engine low to the ground… extra thick oil pan to cut the wind from underneath you. It'll give you thirty or forty more horsepower. I'm gonna give you a fuel line that'll hold an extra gallon of gas. I'm gonna shave half an inch off you and shape you like a bullet. I'll get you primed, painted and weighed, and you'll be ready to go out on that racetrack. Hear me? You're gonna be perfect."*
– Harry Hogge

Knowing how to streamline your taxes can dramatically increase the distance your savings can carry you during retirement. The reason for this is often overlooked by investors who think only in terms of how much their investments can earn. It's equally important to pay attention to how much you are paying out. While everyone has to pay taxes, you don't want to give the government more money than necessary. This is especially important during retirement.

*The amount of money going out every month is equally important as the amount coming in.*

In racing, car builders like Harry Hogge, quoted above, work to properly streamline and fine-tune a vehicle. If an engine is running "too rich," it will burn the fuel too quickly and run out of gas before the end of the track. This can be compared to running out of money before the end of your life.

By simply doing a second review of your taxes, we can make sure you are properly tuned during retirement so the vehicle of your savings takes you distance.

## ARE YOU PAYING YOUR TAXES OR PLANNING FOR THEM?

Everyone is familiar with taxes (you've been paying them your entire working life), but not everyone is familiar with how to make tax planning a part of their retirement strategy.

Taxes are taxes, right? You'll pay them before retirement and you'll pay them during retirement. What's the difference? The truth is that a planful approach to taxes can help you save money, protect your assets and ensure that your legacy remains intact.

How can a tax form do all that? The answer lies in planning. *Tax planning* and *tax reporting* are two very different things. Most people only *report* their taxes. March rolls around, people pull out their 1040s or use TurboTax to enter their income and taxable assets, and ship it off to Uncle Sam at the IRS. If you use a CPA to report your taxes, you are essentially paying them to record history. You have the option of being proactive with your taxes and to plan for your future by making smart, informed decisions about how taxes affect your overall financial plan. Working with a financial professional who, along with a CPA, makes recommendations about your finances to you, will keep you looking forward instead of in the rearview mirror as you enter retirement.

## TAXES AND RETIREMENT

When you retire, you move from the earning and accumulation phase of your life into the asset distribution phase of your life. For most people, that means relying on Social Security, a 401(k), an IRA, or a pension. Wherever you have put your Green Money for retirement, you are going to start relying on it to provide you with the income that once came as a paycheck. Most of these distributions will be considered income by the IRS and will be taxed as such. There are exceptions to that (not all of your Social Security income is taxed, and income from Roth IRAs is not taxed), but for the most part, your distributions will be subject to income taxes.

Regarding assets that you have in an IRA or a 401(k) plan that uses an IRA, when you reach 70 ½ years of age, you will be required to draw a certain amount of money from your IRA as income each year. That amount depends on your age and the balance in your IRA. The amount that you are required to withdraw as income is called a Required Minimum Distribution (RMD). Why are you required to withdraw money from your own account? Chances are the money in that account has grown over time, and the government wants to collect taxes on that growth. If you have a large balance in an IRA, there's a chance your RMD could increase your income significantly enough to put you into a higher tax bracket, subjecting you to a higher tax rate.

Here's where tax planning can really begin to work strongly in your favor. In the distribution phase of your life, you have a predictable income based on your RMDs, your Social Security benefit and any other income-generating assets you may have. What really impacts you at this stage is how much of that money you keep in your pocket after taxes. Essentially, *you will make more money saving on taxes than you will by making more money.* If you can reduce your tax burden by 30, 20 or even 10 percent, you earn yourself that much more money by not paying it in taxes.

How do you save money on taxes? By having a plan. In this instance, a financial professional can work with the CPAs at their firm to create a **distribution plan** that minimizes your taxes and maximizes your annual net income.

## BUILDING A TAX DIVERSIFIED PORTFOLIO

So far so good: avoid taxes, maximize your net annual income and have a plan for doing it. When people decide to leverage the experience and resources of a financial professional, they may not be thinking of how distribution planning and tax planning will benefit their portfolios. Often more exciting prospects like planning income annuities, investing in the market and structuring investments for growth rule the day. Taxes, however, play a crucial role in retirement planning. Achieving those tax goals requires knowledge of options, foresight and professional guidance.

Finding the path to a good tax plan isn't always a simple task. Every tax return you file is different from the one before it because things constantly change. Your expenses change. Planned or unplanned purchases occur. Health care costs, medical bills, an inheritance, property purchases, reaching an age where your RMD kicks in or travel, any number of things can affect how much income you report and how many deductions you take each year.

Preparing for the ever-changing landscape of your financial life requires a tax-diversified portfolio that can be leveraged to balance the incomes, expenditures and deductions that affect you each year. A financial professional will work with you to answer questions like these:

- What does your tax landscape look like?

- Do you have a tax-diversified portfolio robust enough to adapt to your needs?
- Do you have a diversity of taxable and non-taxable income planned for your retirement?
- Will you be able to maximize your distributions to take advantage of your deductions when you retire?
- Is your portfolio strong enough and tax-diversified enough to adapt to an ever-changing (and usually increasing) tax code?

» *When Mimi returns home after a week in the hospital recovering from a knee replacement, the 77-year-old calls her daughter, sister and brother to let them know she is home and feeling well. She also should have called her CPA. Mimi's medical expenses for the procedure, her hospital stay, her medications and the ongoing physical therapy she attended amount to more than $50,000.*

*Currently, Americans can deduct medical expenses that are more than 7.5 percent of their Adjusted Gross Income (AGI). Mimi's AGI is $60,000 the year of her knee replacement, meaning she is able to deduct $44,000 of her medical bills from her taxes that year. Her AGI dictated that she could deduct more than 80 percent of her medical expenses that year.* **Mimi didn't know this**.

*Had she been working with a financial professional who regularly asked her about any changes in her life, her spending, or her expenses (expected or unexpected), Mimi could have saved thousands of dollars. Mimi can also file an amendment to her tax return to recoup the overpayment.*

This relatively simple example of how tax planning can save you money is just the tip of the iceberg. No one can be expected to know the entire U.S. tax code. But a professional who is working with a team of CPAs and financial professionals have an advantage over the average taxpayer who must start from square one on their own every year. Have you been taking advantage of all the deductions that are available to you?

## PROACTIVE TAX PLANNING

The implications of proactive tax planning are far reaching, and are larger than many people realize. Remember, doing your taxes in January, February, March or April means you are writing a history book. Planning your taxes in October, November or December means that you are writing the story as it happens. You can look at all the factors that are at play and make decisions that will impact your tax return *before* you file it.

Realizing that tax planning is an aspect of financial planning is an important leap to make. When you incorporate tax planning into your financial planning strategy, it becomes part of the way you maximize your financial potential. Paying less in taxes means you keep more of your money. Simply put, the more money you keep, the more of it you can leverage as an asset. This kind of planning can affect you at any stage of your life. If you are 40 years old, are you contributing the maximum amount to your 401(k) plan? Are you contributing to a Roth IRA? Are you finding ways to structure the savings you are dedicating to your children's education? Do you have life insurance? Taxes and tax planning affects all of these investment tools. Having a relationship with a professional who works with a CPA can help you build a truly comprehensive financial plan that not only works with your investments, but also shapes your assets to find the most efficient ways to prepare for tax time. There may be years that you could benefit from higher distributions because of the tax bracket that you are in, or there could be years you would benefit from taking less. There may be years when you have a lot of deductions and years you have relatively few. **Adapting your distributions to**

**work in concert with your available deductions** is at the heart of smart tax planning. Professional guidance can bring you to the next level of income distribution, allowing you to remain flexible enough to maximize your tax efficiency. And remember, saving money on taxes makes you more money than making money does. What you have on paper is important: your assets, savings, investments, which are financial expression of your work and time. It's just as important to know how to get it off the paper in a way that keeps most of it in your pocket. Almost anything that involves financial planning also involves taxes. Annuities, investments, IRAs, 401(k)s, 403(b), and many other investment options will have tax implications. Life also has a way of throwing curveballs. Illness, expensive car repair or replacement, or *any event that has a financial impact on your life will likely have a corresponding tax implication* around which you should adapt your financial plan. Tax planning does just that.

**One dollar can end up being less than 25 cents to your heirs.**

» *When Luke's father passed away, he discovered that he was the beneficiary of his father's $500,000 IRA. Luke has a wife and a family of four children, and he knew that his father had intended for a large portion of the IRA to go toward funding their college educations.*

*After Luke's father's estate is distributed, Luke, who is 50 years old and whose two oldest sons are entering college, liquidates the IRA. By doing so, his taxable income for that year puts him in a 39.6 percent tax bracket, immediately reducing the value of the asset to $302,000. An additional 3.8 percent surtax on net investment income further diminishes the funds to $283,000. Liquidating the IRA in effect subjects much of Luke's regular income to the surtax, as well. At this point, Luke will be taxed at 43.4 percent.*

*Luke's state taxes are an additional 9 percent. Moreover, estate taxes on Luke's father's assets claim another 22 percent. By the time the IRS is through, Luke's income from the IRA will be taxed at 75 percent, leaving him with $125,000 of the original $500,000. While it would help contribute to the education of his children, it wouldn't come anywhere near completely paying for it, something the $500,000 could have easily done.*

As the above example makes clear, leaving an asset to your beneficiaries can be more complicated than it may seem. In the case of a traditional IRA, after federal, estate and state taxes, the asset could literally diminish to as little as 25 percent of its value.

How does working with a professional help you make smarter tax decisions with your own finances? Any financial professional worth their salt will be working with a firm that has a team of trained tax professionals, including CPAs, who have an intimate knowledge of the tax code and how to adapt a financial plan to it.

Here's another example of how taxes have major implications on asset management:

> » *Wayne and Kristen, a 62-year-old couple, begin working with a financial professional in October. After structuring their assets to reflect their risk tolerance and creating assets that would provide them Green Money income during retirement, they feel good about their situation. They make decisions that allow them to maximize their Social Security benefits, they have plenty of options for filling their income gap, and have begun a safe yet ambitious Yellow Money strategy with their professional. When their professional asks them about their tax plan, they tell him their CPA handled their taxes every year, and did a great job. Their professional says, "I don't*

*mean who does your taxes, I mean, who does your tax planning?" Wayne and Kristen aren't sure how to respond.*

*Their professional brings Wayne and Kristen's financial plan to the firm's CPA and has her run a tax projection for them. A week later their professional calls them with a tax plan for the year that will save them more than $3,000 on their tax return. The couple is shocked. A simple piece of advice from the CPA based on the numbers revealed that if they paid their estimated taxes before the end of the year, they would be able to itemize it as a deduction, allowing them to save thousands of dollars.*

This solution won't work for everyone, and it may not work for Wayne and Kristen every year. That's not the point. By being proactive with their approach to taxes and using the resources made available by their financial professional, they were able to create a tax plan that saved them money.

## YELLOW MONEY AND TAXES

There are also tax implications for the money that you have managed professionally. People with portions of their investment portfolio that are actively traded can particularly benefit from having a proactive tax strategy. Without going into too much detail, for tax purposes there are two kinds of investment money: qualified and non-qualified. Different investment strategies can have different effects on how you are taxed on your investments and the growth of your investments. Some are more beneficial for one kind of investment strategy over another. Determining how to plan for the taxation of non-qualified and qualified investments is fodder for holiday party discussions at accounting firms. While it may not be a stimulating topic for the average investor, you don't have to understand exactly how it works in order to benefit from it.

While there are many differences between qualified and non-qualified investments, the main difference is this: qualified plans are designed to give investors tax benefits by deferring taxation of their growth until they are withdrawn. Non-qualified investments are not eligible for these deferral benefits. As such, non-qualified investments are taxed whenever income is realized from them in the form of growth.

Actively and non-actively traded investments provide a simple example of how to position your investments for the best tax advantage. In an actively traded and managed portfolio, there is a high amount of buying and selling of stocks, bonds, funds, ETFs, etc. If that active portfolio of non-qualified investments does well and makes a 20 percent return one year and you are in the 39.6 percent tax bracket, your net gain from that portfolio is only about 12 percent (39.6 percent tax of the 20 percent gain is roughly 8 percent.) In a passive trading strategy, you can use a qualified investment tool, such as an IRA, to achieve 13, 14 or 15 percent growth (much lower than the actively traded portfolio), but still realize a higher net return because the growth of the qualified investment is not taxed until it is withdrawn.

Does this mean that you have to always rely on a buy and hold strategy in qualified investment tools? Not necessarily. The question is, if you have qualified and non-qualified investments, where do you want to position your actively traded and managed assets? Incorporating a planful approach to positioning your investments for more beneficial taxation can be done many ways, but let's consider one example. Keeping your actively managed investment strategies inside an IRA or some other qualified plan could allow you to realize the higher gains of those investments without paying tax on their growth every year. Your more passively managed funds could then be kept in taxable, non-qualified vehicles and methods, and because you aren't realizing income from them on an annual basis by frequently trading them, they grow sheltered from taxation.

If you are interested in taking advantage of tax strategies that maximize your net income, you need the attentive strategies, experience and knowledge of a professional who can give you options that position you for profit. At the end of the day, what's important to you as the consumer is how much you keep, your after-tax take home.

## ESTATE TAXES

The government doesn't just tax your income from investments while you're alive. They will also dip into your legacy.

While estate taxes aren't as hot of a topic as they were a few years ago, they are still an issue of concern for many people with assets. While taxes may not apply on estates that are less than $5 million, certain states have estate taxes with much lower exclusion ratios. Some are as low as $600,000. Many people may have to pay a state estate tax. One strategy for avoiding those types of taxes is to move assets outside of your estate. That can include gifting them to family or friends, or putting them into an irrevocable trust. Life insurance is another option for protecting your legacy.

## CHAPTER 10 RECAP //

- When you report your taxes, you are paying to record history. When you *plan* your taxes with a financial professional, you are proactively finding the best options for your tax return.

- It's important to understand the tax repercussions when tapping into assets from a 401(k) or a traditional IRA for use an income source. Money that is considered qualified by the federal government must be taxed upon distribution.

- At the age of 70 ½, the federal government requires all IRA participants to take their RMD, or Required Minimum Distribution. Failure to take your RMD can cost you thousands of dollars in taxes and penalty fees.

- Taxes play an important role during your retirement. It's important that you understand your obligations, and the differences between tax-deferred and tax-advantaged accounts.

- You make more money by saving on taxes than you do by making more money. This simple concept becomes extremely valuable to people in retirement and those living on fixed incomes.

# 11

## FUTURE WEAR
## AND TEAR:
### PLANNING FOR TAX INCREASES

*"There is never enough horsepower... just not enough traction."*
– Carroll Shelby

When racing long distances, the parts of the car stay the same, but
they begin to wear down. If you neglect to address the wear and
tear on these car parts, it has a dramatic effect on the handling
of your vehicle. In the case of your tires, for example, wear and
tear can cause a blow-out that puts an end to your race. This kind
of gradual depletion can be compared to a tax increase and your
ability to pay the bills. During retirement, your income stays essentially the same, but what happens when that income gets worn
down, or depleted, because you have to pay more in taxes? This

chapter taxes a look at the likelihood of future tax increases and what you can do proactively to prevent wear and tear to your retirement.

## THE FUTURE OF U.S. TAXATION

Although the phrase "nothing is certain except for death and taxes" is most famously attributed to Benjamin Franklin, variations of this saying existed even before the country's first taxes were levied, and these words continue to ring true to this day. However, due to recent upheavals in the American financial landscape, this saying might need to be modified to, "nothing is certain except for death and *increasing* taxes."

In the past 10 years alone, the United States has confronted both a debt ceiling and a fiscal cliff, and the federal debt has continued to grow by unprecedented amounts. With the wellbeing of the economy in jeopardy, legislation regarding debt reduction and tax reform has become a hot button issue. Regardless of which legislation has been, or will be, thrown at the American public, the truth of the matter remains the same: the country's current tax revenues cannot cover its obligations.

If the government wants to keep the lights on, it's going to need more income, which not only means that you can count on being taxed, but also on being taxed at an increasing rate.

## DEBT CEILING – CAUSE AND EFFECTS

Since 2000, Congress has raised the debt ceiling more than a dozen times. Increasing the debt ceiling is needed because the government keeps maxing out its credit limit, which it has been reliant upon since the beginning of the Industrial Revolution. Essentially, each time the federal government reaches the end of its line of credit; Congress raises the debt ceiling to extend it. This type of poor money management behavior is nothing new for many Americans: many people overuse their credit cards and rack up an impressive amount of debt. However, most people do not have the ability to raise the credit limit on a card once they have maxed it out—unless they can show they have the ability to pay the balance back. The only way to pay a credit line back is by making more money than you're spending. In other words, responsibility and a balanced budget are critical components to repaying a debt.

The federal government keeps finding ways to increase its credit line without also finding ways to proportionally cut its spending. Although some spending cuts have been put in place, they are not large enough to be worthy adversaries of the current debt situation. Consequently, the continual increasing of the debt ceiling has raised more than just the ability of the federal government to go further into debt; it has also raised concerns and fears about the direction in which the economy is heading. As investors' worry about the impact that future investment valuations may have on their personal wealth grows progressively serious, the market continues to swing unpredictably.

The truth of the matter is that raising the debt ceiling is only one part of the equation required to address the country's debt problem—tax reform is the other. If the government wants to try to staunch the flow of its ever-rising debt, then it will need to make more money, and the only way the government makes money is by collecting taxes. Unfortunately, however, the government frequently collects less than it spends: the Congressional Budget Office (CBO) estimated the 2017 budget deficit would be $559 billion.*

## DEBT AND EARNINGS

Currently, the national debt is increasing at an unprecedented rate, rising to levels never seen before and threatening serious harm

---

* *https://www.cbo.gov/publication/52370*

to the economy. In October 2004, the national debt was $7.4 trillion*, and by April 2017 it had climbed to nearly $20 trillion**, which means the national debt grew 270.3 percent during this time period. To further understand the gravity of this situation, consider that economists believe that a sustainable economy's debt exists at a maximum level of approximately 80 percent. In 2014, the U.S. national debt was 101.8 percent of the GDP.*** By 2017, the U.S. national debt has risen to 104.3 percent of the GDP.****

The significance of these two numbers lies within the contrast. The national debt is the amount that needs to be repaid; this can be thought of as the government's credit card balance. The GDP represents the market value of all goods and services produced within a country during a given period. In other words, the GDP represents the gross taxable income available to the government. If debts are increasing at a rate greater than the gross income available for taxation, then the only way to make up the difference is to increase the rate at which the gross income is being taxed.

Even more concerning is that the disparity between growth in national debt and growth in GDP is projected to continue, which means the amount of money the federal government owes will far outpace its ability to repay it. As anyone who has struggled with debt can tell you, continually borrowing more money than you make can have potentially disastrous consequences.

Unfortunately, analysis of the federal government's budget also shows that regardless of revenue collection rates and increased taxes, the deficit will most likely continue to increase, and without

---

* CBO, An Update to the Budget and Economic Outlook: 2014 - 2024

** US Department of the Treasury's Bureau of the Fiscal Service, www.treasurydirect.gov/NP/debt/current

*** Federal Reserve Bank of St Louis Economic Research

**** Federal Reserve Bank of St Louis Economic Research, https://fred.stlouisfed.org/series/GFDEGDQ188S

additional spending cuts to help bring the budget into balance, tax increases are likely to continue.

## THE END OF AN ERA

From a historical point of view, taxes are extremely low. The last time the U.S. national debt was even close to the same percentage level of GDP as it is today was for several years after the end of World War II. The maximum tax rate at that point, and through the years from 1944 through 1963, averaged 90 percent. Compare that to the maximum rate of 39.6 percent today, and it becomes very clear that there is a disparity of extreme proportion.

Taxes during this historical period were at extreme levels for nearly 20 years, throughout and following this level of debt-to-GDP. A significant point to note about the difference at that time versus where we are today is the economic activity. The period of 1944 through 1963 was in the heart of both the Industrial Revolution and the birth of the baby-boom generation. Today, we are mired in extreme volatility with frequent periods of boom and bust accompanied by the beginning of the greatest retirement wave ever experienced within the U.S. economy.

To contrast these two time periods with respect to the recovery period is almost asinine, as the external pressures from globalization and domestic unfunded liabilities did not exist or were irrelevant factors during the prior period.

To add insult to injury, U.S. domestic unfunded liabilities were estimated to be about $84 trillion in 2012 and that number has only increased through the intervening years*. These liabilities exist outside of the annual budgetary debt discussed above and are due to items such as Social Security, Medicare and government pensions. The most concerning part of this stems from the fact

---

* *National Center for Policy Analysis, How Much Does the Federal Government Owe?,* June 2012

that we are on the cusp of the greatest retirement wave in U.S. history as the baby-boom generation begins retiring and drawing from the unfunded Social Security for which they currently have entitlement. Over the long-run, expenditures related to healthcare programs such as Medicare and Medicaid are projected to grow faster than the economy overall as the population matures.

To put unfunded liabilities into perspective, consider these as off-balance-sheet obligations similar to those of Enron. Although these are not listed as part of the national debt, they must be paid just the same. The difference between Enron and the U.S. unfunded liabilities is that if the U.S. government cannot come up with the funds to pay all these liabilities through revenue generation then they will print the money necessary to pay the debt.

## WHAT DOES THE SOLUTION LOOK LIKE?

Unfortunately, the general public is in a no-win situation for this solution to the problem. Printing money does not bode well for economic growth as this action creates inflationary pressures that devalue the U.S. dollar and make everyone less wealthy. Cutting the entitlements that compose this liability leaves millions of people without benefits they have come to expect. The only other option, and one that the government knows all too well, is increased taxes. In fact, according to a Congressional Budget Office paper issued in 2004\*, unfunded liabilities are addressed as follows:

*"The term 'unfunded liability' has been used to refer to a gap between the government's projected financial commitment under a particular program and the revenues that are expected to be available to fund that commitment. But no government obligation can be*

---

\* CBO paper, *Measures of the U.S. Government's Fiscal Position Under Current Law,* Sept. 2004

*truly considered 'unfunded' because of the U.S. government's sovereign
power to tax—which is the ultimate resource to meet its obligations."*

A balanced budget is going to be required at some point and
with this will come higher taxes. Given our current position and
projected budgets, it is likely that tax increases are coming in the
near future. However, although raising taxes is a strategy to raise
money, it is not a solution to the government's current and pend-
ing fiscal problems.

How do you prepare? Why spend so much time reassuring
you that taxes will increase? Because you have an opportunity to
take action. Now is the time to prepare for what is to come by
structuring countermeasures for the good, the bad, and the ugly
of each of these legislative nightmares through tax-advantaged
retirement planning.

The truth of the matter is that you make more money by saving on taxes than you do by making more money. The simplistic
logic of this statement makes sense when you discover it takes a
$1.50 in earnings to put that same dollar, saved in taxes, back in
your pocket.* This simple concept becomes extremely valuable to
people in retirement and those living on fixed incomes.

As simple as it sounds, it is much more difficult to execute.
Most people fail to put together a plan as they near retirement,
beginning with a simple cash flow budget. If you have not ana-
lyzed your proposed income streams and expenses, you could not
possibly have taken the time to position these cash flows and other
events into a tax-preferred plan.

Most people will state, "I have a plan" and thus, they do not
need any further assistance in this area. The truth in most instances
is that many of these people could not show you their plan, and
of the few that could, they would not be able to show you how
they have executed it. In this regard, they may as well be Richard

---

* *Assuming a 33 percent effective tax rate*

Nixon saying, "I am not a crook" for as much as they claim, "I have a plan." The truth lies in waiting.

As you approach or begin retirement, you should look at what cash flows you will have. Do you have a pension? How about Social Security? How much additional cash flow are you going to need to draw from your assets to maintain the lifestyle that you desire?

Most people spend their whole lives saving and accumulating wealth but very little time determining a strategy that will distribute this accumulation in ways that will help them to retain it. You need to make sure you have the appropriate diversification of taxable versus non-taxable assets to complement your distribution strategy.

## THE BENEFITS OF DIVERSIFICATION

Heading into retirement, you should be situated within a diversified tax landscape. The point to spending your whole life accumulating wealth is not to see how big the number is on paper, but rather to be an exercise in how much you put in your pocket after removing it from the paper.

To truly understand tax diversification, you must understand what types of money exist and how each of these will be treated during accumulation and, most importantly, during distribution. The following is a brief summary:

1. Free money
2. Tax-advantaged money
3. Tax-deferred money
4. Taxable money
   a. Ordinary income
   b. Capital gains and qualified dividends

## FREE MONEY

Free money is the best kind of money regardless of the tax treatment, because in the end you have more money than you would have otherwise. Many employers will provide contributions toward employee retirement accounts to offer additional employment benefits and inspire employees to save for their own retirement. With this, employers often will offer a matching contribution in which they will contribute up to a certain percentage of an employee's salary, generally three to five percent, to that employee's retirement account when the employee contributes to their retirement account as well. For example, if an employee earns $50,000 annually and contributes three percent ($1,500) to their retirement account annually, the employer will also contribute three percent ($1,500) to the employee's account. That is $1,500 in free money. Take all that you can get!

## TAX-ADVANTAGED MONEY

Tax-advantaged money is the next best thing to free-money. Although you have to earn tax-advantaged money you do not have to give part of it away to Uncle Sam. Tax-advantaged money comes in three basic forms that you can utilize during your lifetime; four if prison inspires your future, but it's not necessary to discuss that option.

One of the most commonly known forms of tax-advantaged money is municipal bonds, which earn and pay interest that could be federally tax-advantaged, state tax-advantaged, or both state and federal tax-advantaged. There are several caveats that should be discussed in regard to the notion of tax-advantaged income from municipal bonds. First, you will notice that tax-advantaged has several flavors from the state and federal perspective. This is because states will generally tax the interest earned on a municipal bond unless the bond is offered from an entity located within that state. This severely limits the availability of completely tax-advantaged municipal bonds and constrains underlying risk and liquidity factors. Second, municipal bond interest gets added back into the equation for determining your modified adjusted gross income (MAGI) for Social Security and could push your income above the thresholds subjecting a portion of your Social Security income to taxation. In effect, if this interest subjects some other income to taxation then this interest is truly being taxed. Last, municipal bond interest may be excluded from the regular federal tax system, but it is included for determining tax under the alternative minimum tax (AMT) system. In its basic form, the AMT system is a separate tax system that applies if the tax computed under AMT exceeds the tax computed under the regular tax system, the difference between these two computations is the alternative minimum tax.

## TAX-FREE MONEY: ROTH IRA

Roth accounts are probably the single greatest tax asset that has come from Congress outside of life insurance and are well known but rarely used. Roth IRAs were first established by the Taxpayer Relief Act of 1997 and were named after Senator William Roth, the chief sponsor of the legislation. A Roth account is simply an account in the form of an IRA or an employer-sponsored retirement account that allows for tax-advantaged growth of earnings and, thus, tax-advantaged income.

The main difference between a Roth and a traditional IRA or employer-sponsored plan lies within the timing of the taxation. You're probably very familiar with the typical scenario of putting money away for retirement through an employer plan, whereby your employer deducts money from each paycheck and puts it directly into a retirement account. This money is taken out before taxes are calculated meaning you do not pay tax on those earnings today. A Roth account, on the other hand, takes the money *after* the taxes have been taken out and then puts it into the retirement account, so you do pay tax on the money today. The other significant difference between these two is taxation during distribution in later years. With a traditional retirement account, when you take the money out later it gets added to your ordinary income and is taxed accordingly. Additionally, including this in your income subjects you to the consequences previously mentioned for municipal bonds with Social Security taxation, AMT, as well as higher Medicare premiums. A Roth, on the other hand, has tax-advantaged distributions and does not contribute toward negative impact items such as Social Security taxation, AMT, or Medicare premium increases. It essentially comes back to you without tax and other obligations.

The best way to consider the difference between the two accounts is to look at the life of a farmer. A farmer will buy seed, plant it in the ground, grow the crops, and harvest it later for sale. Typically, the farmer would only pay tax on the crops that have been harvested and sold. But if you were the farmer, would you rather pay tax on $5,000 worth of seed that you plant today or $50,000 worth of harvested crop later? The obvious answer is $5,000 worth of seed today. The truth of the matter is that you are a farmer, except you are planting dollars into your retirement account instead of seeds into the earth.

So why doesn't everyone have a Roth retirement account if things are so simple? There are several reasons, but the single greatest reason has been the constraints on contributions. If you earned over certain thresholds (MAGI over $133,000 single and $196,000 joint for 2017), you were not eligible to make contributions, and, until 2010, if your modified adjusted gross income (MAGI) was over $100,000 (single or joint) then you could not convert a traditional IRA to a Roth. Outside of these contribution limits, most people save for retirement through their employers and most employers are not offering Roth options within their plans. The reason behind this is because Roth accounts are not that well understood and people have been educated to believe that saving on taxes today is the best possible course of action.

## TAX-FREE MONEY: LIFE INSURANCE

As previously mentioned, the single greatest tax asset that has come from Congress outside of life insurance is the Roth account. Life insurance is the little known or discussed tax asset that holds some of the greatest value for your financial history both during life and upon death, and it is by far the best tax-advantaged device available. Traditionally, life insurance is viewed as a way to protect your loved ones from financial ruin upon your demise and it should be noted that everyone who cares about someone should have life insurance. By purchasing a life insurance policy, your loved ones will be assured a financial windfall from the life insurance company when you die that will help them with your final expenses and carry on their lives without you comfortably. The best part about the life insurance windfall is the fact that nobody will have to pay tax on the money received. This is the single greatest tax-advantaged device available, but it has one downside, you do not get to use it. Only your heirs will.

The little known and discussed part of life insurance is the cash value build-up within whole life and universal life (permanent) policies. Life insurance is not typically seen as an investment vehicle for building wealth and retirement planning, although it should briefly be discussed why this thought process should be re-evaluated. Permanent life insurance is generally misconceived as something that is very expensive for a wealth accumulation vehicle as there are mortality charges (fees for the death benefit) that detract from the returns that are available and further, those returns do not yield as much as the stock market over the long run. This is why many times you will hear the phrase "buy term and invest the rest," where "term" refers to term insurance.

It's important to review the two terms just used in regard to life insurance: term and permanent. Term insurance is what most people are familiar with. You purchase a certain death benefit that will go to your heirs upon your death and this policy will be in effect for a certain number of years, typically 10 to 20 years. The 10 to 20 years is the term of the policy and once you have reached that end you no longer have insurance unless you purchase another policy at that point.

On the other hand, permanent insurance has no term involved, it is permanent as long as the premiums continue to be paid. Permanent insurance generally has higher premiums than term insurance for the same amount of death benefit coverage and it is this difference that is referred to when people say "invest the rest."

Simply speaking, there are significant differences between these two policies that do not get taken into consideration when providing a comparative analysis in the numbers. One item that gets lost in the fray when comparing term and permanent insurance is that term usually expires before death, in fact insurance studies show less than 1 percent of all term policies pay out death benefit claims. The issue arises when the term expires and the desire to have more insurance is still present. A term policy with the same benefit will be much more expensive than the original policy and, many times, life events occur, such as cancer or heart conditions, which makes it impossible to acquire another policy and leaves your loved ones unprotected and tax-advantaged legacy planning out of the equation.

Another aspect and probably the most important piece in consideration of the future of taxation is the fact that permanent insurance has a cash accumulation value. Two aspects stand out with the cash accumulation value. First, as the cash accumulation value increases the death benefit will also increase whereas term insurance is level. Second, this cash accumulation offers value to you during your lifetime rather than just your heirs upon death.

The cash accumulation value can be used for tax-advantaged income during your lifetime through policy loans. Most importantly, this tax-advantaged income is available during retirement for distribution planning, all while offering the same typical financial protection to your heirs.

## TAX-DEFERRED MONEY

Tax-deferred money is the type of money from which most people are familiar, but the idea was also briefly reviewed above. Tax-deferred money is typically your traditional IRA, employer sponsored retirement plan, or a non-qualified annuity. Essentially, money is put into an investment vehicle that will accumulate in value over time and you do not pay taxes on the earnings that grow in these accounts until it is distributed. Taxes must be paid once the money is distributed and, in addition to the taxes, the same negative consequences exist toward additional taxation and expense in other areas as previously discussed.

## TAXABLE MONEY

Taxable money is everything else and is taxable both today and later, whenever it is received.

Of these four types of money, they really come down to two distinct classifications: taxable and tax-advantaged.

The greatest difference when comparing taxable and tax-advantaged income is a function of how much money you will keep after tax. For help in determining what the differences should be, excluding outside factors such as Social Security taxation and AMT, a tax equivalent yield should be used.

## TAX-FREE IN THE REAL WORLD

To put the tax equivalent yield into perspective, consider the following example:

» *Bob and Mary are currently retired and in the 25 percent tax bracket living on Social Security and interest from investments. They have a substantial portion of their investments in municipal bonds yielding 6 percent, which in today's market is quite comforting. The tax equivalent yield they would need to earn from a taxable investment would be 8 percent, a 2 percent gap which seems almost impossible given current market volatility. However, something that has never been put into perspective is that the interest from their municipal bonds is subject to taxation on their Social Security benefits\* (at 21.25 percent). With this, the yield on their municipal bonds would be 4.725 percent\*\*, and the taxable equivalent yield falls to 6.3 percent leaving a gap of only 1.575 percent.*

In the end, most people spend their lives accumulating wealth through the best, if not only vehicle they know, a tax-deferred account. This account is most likely a 401(k) or 403(b) plan offered through your employer and may be supplemented with an IRA that was established at one point or another. As the years go by, people blindly throw money into these accounts in an effort to save for a retirement that they someday hope to reach.

The truth is most people have an age selected for when they would like to retire but spend their lives wondering if they will ever be able to actually quit working. To answer this question, you must understand how much money you will have available to contribute toward your needs. In other words, you need to know what your after-tax income will be during this period.

All else being equal, it would not matter if you put your money into a taxable, tax-deferred, or tax-advantaged account as long as

---

\* *Assuming each dollar of interest subjects a dollar of Social Security income to taxation at 85 percent*

\*\* *6.0 percent − (6.0 percent -21.25 percent) = 4.725 percent* income tax rates never change and outside factors are never an event. The net amount you receive in the end will be the same. Unfortunately, this will never be the case. We already know that taxes will increase in the future, meaning we will likely see higher taxes in retirement than during our peak earning years.

Regardless, saving for retirement in any form is a good thing since it appears from all practical perspectives that future government benefits will be cut and taxes will increase. You have the ability to plan today for efficient tax diversification and maximization of your after-tax dollars during your distribution years.

## CHAPTER 11 RECAP //

- The future of U.S. taxation is uncertain. You know what the tax rate and landscape is today, but you won't tomorrow. The only thing you can really count on is the trend of increasing taxation.
- You make more money by saving on taxes than you do by making more money. This simple concept becomes extremely valuable to people in retirement and those living on fixed incomes.

# 12

## HOW TO AVOID
## THE BENDS:
### ROTH IRA CONVERSION

*"Scuba diving is very much a black and white world in terms
of the laws and rules one must abide by. It comes down to
clear and cut physics. If the laws are broken, severe penalties
are exacted, including paralysis or even death."*
– Carlos Eyes, *The Blue Edge*

In deep sea diving, a serious condition known as the bends, or
decompression sickness, has prompted the rule: never come up
quicker than your slowest bubble. When rising to the surface after
being deep under water, the nitrogen in your blood expands, and
it can cause an embolism in your brain or blood stream that can
kill you. While it might be a bit dramatic to say that an increase

in taxes can kill you, it's fair to make the comparison here by saying that having to shoulder an increasing tax burden can be debilitating to someone who is essentially unemployed. Think of it this way:

If you have a traditional IRA, what you have is essentially a big pool of untaxed money. The attractive qualities of Roth IRAs may have prompted you to explore the possibility of moving some of your assets into a Roth account. As you know, any money withdrawn from a Roth IRA is tax free. Converting the money in a traditional IRA means paying today's tax rate, which is likely to save you thousands of dollars in the future. The trick to doing this Roth IRA conversion is, like deep sea diving, all about the timing. You don't want to go too slow or too fast when converting your tax burden. There are artful strategies your financial professional can employ to help lessen the load. For example, making the conversion during a low-income earning year can work to your benefit. Before we go into the timing and mechanics of a conversion, the moral question of its efficacy is addressed by an Associate Justice on the Supreme Court of the United States, Louis Brandeis, who served from 1916 to 1939.

## TAKE THE FREE BRIDGE

Louis Brandeis provides one of the best examples illustrating how tax planning works. Born in Louisville, Kentucky, Brandeis was an intelligent man with a touch of country charm. He described tax planning this way:

*"I live in Alexandria, Virginia. Near the Court Chambers, there is a toll bridge across the Potomac. When in a rush, I pay the dollar toll and get home early. However, I usually drive outside the downtown section of the city and cross the Potomac on a free bridge.*

*The bridge was placed outside the downtown Washington, D.C. area to serve a useful social service—getting drivers to drive the extra mile and help alleviate congestion during the rush hour.*

*If I went over the toll bridge and through the barrier without paying a toll, I would be committing tax evasion.*

*If I drive the extra mile and drive outside the city of Washington to the free bridge, I am using a legitimate, logical and suitable method of tax avoidance, and I am performing a useful social service by doing so.*

*The tragedy is that **few people know that the free bridge exists**."*

Like Brandeis, most American taxpayers have options when it comes to "crossing the Potomac," so to speak. It's a financial planner's job to tell you what options are available. You can wait until March to file your taxes, at which time you might pay someone to report and pay the government a larger portion of your income. However, you could instead file before the end of the year, work with your financial professional and incorporate a tax plan as part of your overall financial planning strategy. Filing later is like crossing the toll bridge. Tax planning is like crossing the free bridge.

Which would you rather do?

The answer to this question is easy. Most people want to save money and pay less in taxes. What makes this situation really difficult in real life, however, is that the signs along the side of the road that direct us to the free bridge are not that clear. To normal Americans, and to plenty of people who have studied it, the U.S. tax code is easy to get lost in. There are all kinds of rules, exceptions to rules, caveats and conditions that are difficult to understand, or even to know about. What you really need to know is your options and the bottom line impacts of those options.

## ROTH IRA CONVERSIONS

One important difference between the traditional and Roth accounts is how they treat Required Minimum Distributions (RMDs). When you turn 70 ½ years old, you are required to take a minimum amount of money out of a traditional IRA. This amount is your RMD. It is treated as taxable income. Roth IRAs, however, do not have RMDs, and their distributions are not taxable. Quite a deal, right?

While having a Roth IRA as part of your portfolio is a good idea, converting assets to a Roth IRA can pose some challenges, depending on what kinds of assets you want to transfer.

One common option is the conversion of a traditional IRA to a Roth IRA. You may have heard about converting your IRA to a Roth IRA, but you might not know the full net result on your income. The main difference between the two accounts is that the growth of investments within a traditional IRA is not taxed until income is withdrawn from the account, whereas taxes are charged on contribution amounts to a Roth IRA, not withdrawals. The problem, however, is that when assets are removed from a traditional IRA, even if the assets are being transferred to a Roth IRA account, taxes apply.

There are a lot of reasons to look at Roth conversions. People have a lot of money in IRAs, up to multiple millions of dollars. Even with $500,000, when they turn 70 ½ years old, their RMD is going to be approximately $18,000, and they have to take that out whether they want to or not. It's a tax issue. Essentially, if you will be subject to high RMDs, it could have impacts on how much of your Social Security is taxable, and on your tax bracket.

By paying taxes now instead of later on assets in a Roth IRA, you can realize tax-advantaged growth. You pay once and you're done paying. Your heirs are done paying. It's a powerful tool. Here's a simple example to show you how powerful it can be:

*Imagine that you pay to convert a traditional IRA to a Roth. You have decided that you want to put the money in a vehicle that gives you a tax-advantaged income option down the road. If you pay a 25 percent tax on that conversion and the Roth IRA then doubles in value over the next 10 years, you could look at your situation as only having paid 12.5 percent tax.*

The prospect of tax-advantaged income is a tempting one. While you have to pay a conversion tax to transfer your assets, you also have turned taxable income into tax free retirement money that you can let grow as long as you want without being required to withdraw it.

There are options, however, that address this problem. Much like the Brandeis story, there may be a "free bridge" option for many investors.

Your financial professional will likely tell you that it is not a matter of whether or not you should perform a Roth IRA conversion, it is a matter of how much you should convert and when.

Here are some of the things to consider before converting to a Roth IRA:

- If you make a conversion before you retire, you may end up paying higher taxes on the conversion because it is likely that you are in some of your highest earning years, placing you in the highest tax bracket of your life. It is possible that a better strategy would be to wait until after you retire, a time when you may have less taxable income, which would place you in a lower tax bracket.

- Many people opt to reduce their work hours from fulltime to part-time in the years before they retire. If you have pursued this option, your income will likely be lower, in turn lowering your tax rate.

- The first years that you draw Social Security benefits can also be years of lower reported income, making it another good time frame in which to convert to a Roth IRA.

One key strategy to handling a Roth IRA conversion is to *always be able to pay the cost of the tax conversion with outside money.* Structuring your tax year to include something like a significant deduction can help you offset the conversion tax. This way you aren't forced to take the money you need for taxes from the value of the IRA. The reason taxes apply to this maneuver is because when you withdraw money from a traditional IRA, it is treated as taxable income by the IRS. Your financial professional, with the help of the CPAs at their firm, may be able to provide you with options like after-tax money, itemized deductions or other situations that can pose effective tax avoidance options.

Some examples of avoiding Roth IRA conversions taxes include:

- *Using medical expenses that are above 10 percent of your Adjusted Gross Income.* If you have health care costs that you can list as itemized deductions, you can convert an amount of income from a traditional IRA to a Roth IRA that is offset by the deductible amount. Essentially, deductible medical expenses negate the taxes resulting from recording the conversion.

- *Individuals, usually small business owners, who are dealing with a Net Operating Loss (NOL).* If you have NOLs, but aren't able to utilize all of them on your tax return, you can carry them forward to offset the taxable income from the taxes on income you convert to a Roth IRA.

- *Charitable giving.* If you are charitably inclined, you can use the amount of your donations to reduce the amount of taxable income you have during that year. By matching the amount you convert to a Roth IRA to the amount your taxable income was reduced by charitable giving, you can essentially avoid taxation on the conversion. You may decide to double your donations to a charity in one year, giving them two years' worth of donations in order to offset the Roth IRA conversion tax on this year's tax return.

- *Investments that are subject to depletion.* Certain investments can kick off depletion expenses. If you make an investment and are subject to depletion expenses, they can be deducted and used to offset a Roth IRA conversion tax.

Not all of the above scenarios work for everyone, and there are many other options for offsetting conversion taxes. The point is that you have options, and your financial professional and tax professional can help you understand those options.

If you have a traditional IRA, Roth conversions are something you should look at. As you approach retirement you should consider your options and make choices that keep more of your money in your pocket, not the government's.

## ADDITIONAL TAX BENEFITS OF ROTH IRAS

Not only do Roth IRAs provide you with tax-advantaged growth, they also give you a tax diversified landscape that allows you to maximize your distributions. Chances are that no matter the circumstances, you will have taxed income and other assets subject to taxation. *But if you have a Roth IRA, you have the unique ability to manage your Adjusted Gross Income (AGI), because you have a tax-advantaged income option!*

Converting to a Roth IRA can also help you preserve and build your legacy. Because Roth IRAs are exempt from RMDs, after you make a conversion from a traditional IRA, your Roth account can grow tax-advantaged for another 15, 20 or 25 years and it can be used as tax-advantaged income by your heirs. It is important to note, however, that non-spousal beneficiaries do have to take RMDs from a Roth IRA, or choose to stretch it and draw tax-advantaged income out of it over their lifetime.

## TO CONVERT OR NOT TO CONVERT?

Conversions aren't only for retirees. You can convert at any time. Your choice should be based on your individual circumstances and tax situation. Sticking with a traditional IRA or converting to a Roth, again, depends on your individual circumstances, including your income, your tax bracket and the amount of deductions you have each year.

Is it better to have a Roth IRA or traditional IRA? It depends on your individual circumstance. Some people don't mind having taxable income from an IRA. Their income might not be very high and their RMD might not bump their tax bracket up, so it's not as big a deal. A similar situation might involve income from Social Security. Social Security benefits are taxed based on other income you are drawing. If you are in a position where none or very little of your Social Security benefit is subject to taxes, paying income tax on your RMD may be very easy.

> » *There are also situations where leveraging taxable income from a traditional IRA can work to your advantage come tax time. Russell and Jennifer, for example, dream of buying a boat when they retire. It is something they have looked forward to their entire marriage. In addition to the savings and investments that they created to supply them with income during retirement, which includes a traditional IRA, they have also saved money for the sole purpose of purchasing a boat once they stop working.*
>
> *When the time comes and they finally buy the boat of their dreams, they pay an additional $15,000 in sales taxes that year because of the large purchase. Because they are retired and earning less money, the deductions they used to be able to realize from their income taxes are no longer there. The high amount of sales taxes they paid on the boat puts them in a*

*position where they could benefit from taking taxable income from a traditional IRA.*

*When Russell and Jennifer's financial professional learns about their purchase, he immediately contacts a CPA at his firm to run the numbers. They determine that by taking a $15,000 distribution from their IRA, they could fulfill their income needs to offset the $15,000 sales tax deduction that they were claiming due to the purchase of their boat. In the end, they pay zero taxes on their income distribution from their IRA.*

The moral of the story? **Having a tax diversified landscape gives you options.** Having capital assets that can be liquidated, tax-advantaged income options and sources that can create capital gains or capital losses will put you in a position to play your cards right no matter what you want to accomplish with your taxes. The ace up your sleeve is your financial professional and the CPAs they work with. Do yourself a favor and *plan* your taxes instead of *reporting* them!

## CHAPTER 12 RECAP //

- Given that the future of U.S. taxation is certain to bring an increase, a Roth IRA Conversion allows you to pay your taxes ahead of time while in a lower tax bracket.
- Look for the "free bridge" option in your tax strategy.
- Converting from a traditional to a Roth IRA can provide you with tax-advantaged retirement income.
- Converting to a Roth IRA can also help you preserve and build your legacy.
- There are many ways to reduce your taxes. Being smart about your Roth IRA conversion is one of the main ways to do so.

# 13

# YOUR LEGACY BEYOND DOLLARS AND CENTS

*"The reason we race isn't so much to beat each other...*
*but to be with each other."*
– Christopher McDougall, *Born to Run*

If you're like most people, planning your estate isn't on the top of your list of things to do. Planning your income needs for retirement, managing your assets and just living your life without worrying about how your estate will be handled when you are gone make legacy planning less than attractive for a Saturday afternoon task. The fact of the matter, however, is that if you don't plan your legacy, someone else will. That someone else is usually a combination of the IRS and other government entities: lawyers, executors, courts, and accountants. Who do you think has the best interests of your beneficiaries in mind?

Today, there is more consideration given to planning a legacy than just maximizing your estate. When most people think about an estate, it may seem like something only the very wealthy have: a stately manor or an enormous business. But a legacy is something else entirely. A legacy is more than the sum total of the financial assets you have accumulated. It is the lasting impression you make on those you leave behind. The dollar and cents are just a small part of a legacy.

- A legacy encompasses the stories that others tell about you, shared experiences and values. An estate may pay for college tuition, but a legacy may inform your grandchildren about the importance of higher education and self-reliance.

- A legacy may also contain family heirlooms or items of emotional significance. It may be a piece of art your great-grandmother painted, family photos, or a childhood keepsake.

When you go about planning your legacy, certainly explore strategies that can maximize the financial benefit to the ones you care about. But also take the time to ensure that you have organized the whole of your legacy, and let that be a part of the last gift you leave.

Many people avoid planning their legacy until they feel they must. Something may change in your life, like the birth of a grandchild, the diagnosis of a serious health problem, or the death of a close friend or loved one. Waiting for tragedy to strike in order to get your affairs in order is not the best course of action. The emotional stress of that kind of situation can make it hard to make patient, thoughtful decisions. Taking the time to create a premeditated and thoughtful legacy plan will assure that your assets will be transferred where and when you want them when the time comes.

## THE BENEFITS OF PLANNING YOUR LEGACY

The distribution of your assets, whether in the form of property, stocks, Individual Retirement Accounts, 401(k)s or liquid assets, can be a complicated undertaking if you haven't left clear instructions about how you want them handled. Not having a plan will cost more money and take more time, leaving your loved ones to wait (sometimes for years) and receive less of your legacy than if you had a clear plan.

Planning your legacy will help your assets be transferred with little delay and little confusion. Instead of leaving decisions about how to distribute your estate to your family, attorneys or financial professionals, preserve your legacy and your wishes by drafting a clear plan at an early age.

And while you know all that, it can still be hard to sit down and do it. It reminds you that life is short, and the relatively complicated nature of sorting through your assets can feel like a daunting task. But one thing is for sure: *it is impossible for your assets to be transferred or distributed the way you want at the end of your life if you don't have a plan.*

Ask yourself:

- Are my assets up to date?
- Have my primary and contingent beneficiaries been clearly designated?
- Does my plan allow for restriction of a beneficiary?
- Does my legacy plan address minor children that I want to provide with income?
- Does my legacy plan allow for multi-generational payout?

Answers to these questions are critical if you want the final say in how your assets are distributed. In order to achieve your legacy goals, you need a plan.

## MAKING A PLAN

Eventually, when your income need is filled and you have sufficient standby money to meet your need for emergencies, travel or other extra expenses you are planning for, whatever isn't used during your lifetime becomes your financial legacy. The money that you do not use during your lifetime will either go to loved ones, unloved ones, charity, or the IRS. The question is, who would you rather disinherit?

By having a legacy plan that clearly outlines your assets, your beneficiaries and your distribution goals, you can make sure that your money and property is ending up in the hands of the people you determine beforehand. Is it really that big of a deal? It absolutely is. Think about it. Without a clear plan, it is impossible for anyone to know if your beneficiary designations are current and reflect your wishes because you haven't clearly expressed who your beneficiaries are. You may have an idea of who you want your assets to go to, but without a plan, it is anyone's guess. It is also impossible to know if the titling of your assets is accurate unless you have gone through and determined whose name is on the titles. More importantly, *if you have not clearly and effectively communicated your desires regarding the planned distribution of your legacy, you and your family may end up losing a large part of it.*

As you can see, managing a legacy is more complicated than having an attorney read your will, divide your estate and write checks to your heirs. The additional issue of taxes, Family Maximum Benefit calculations and a host of other decisions rear their heads. Educating yourself about the best options for positioning your legacy assets is a challenging undertaking. Working with a financial professional who is versed in determining the most efficient and effective ways of preserving and distributing your legacy can save you time, money and strife.

So, how do you begin?

**Making a Legacy Plan Starts with a Simple List.** The first, and one of the largest, steps to setting up an estate plan with a financial professional that reflects your desires is creating a detailed inventory of your assets and debts (if you have any). You need to know what assets you have, who the beneficiaries are, how much they are worth and how they are titled. You can start by identifying and listing your assets. This is a good starting point for working with a financial professional who can then help you determine the detailed information about your assets that will dictate how they are distributed upon your death.

If you are particularly concerned about leaving your kids and grandkids a lifetime of income with minimal taxes, you will want to discuss a Stretch IRA option with your financial professional.

## STRETCH IRAS: GETTING THE MOST OUT OF YOUR MONEY

In 1986, the U.S. Congress passed a law that allows for multi-generational distributions of IRA assets. This type of distribution is called a Stretch IRA because it stretches the distribution of the account out over a longer period of time to several beneficiaries. It also allows the account to continue accumulating value throughout your relatives' lifetimes. You can use a Stretch IRA as an income tool that distributes throughout your lifetime, your children's lifetimes and your grandchildren's lifetimes.

Stretch IRAs are an attractive option for those more concerned with creating income for their loved ones than leaving them with a lump sum that may be subject to a high tax rate. With traditional IRA distributions, non-spousal beneficiaries must generally take distributions from their inherited IRAs, whether transferred or not, within five years after the death of the IRA owner. An exception to this rule applies if the beneficiary elects to take distributions over his or her lifetime, which is referred to as stretching the IRA.

Let's begin by looking at the potential of stretching an IRA throughout multiple generations.

> *» In this scenario, Mr. Cleaver has an IRA with a current balance of $350,000. If we assume a five percent annual rate of return, and a 28% tax rate, the Stretch IRA turned*

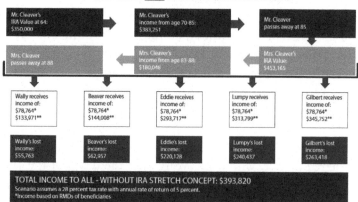

*a $502,625 legacy into more than $1.5 million. Doubling the value of the IRA also provided Mr. Cleaver, his wife, two children and three grandchildren with income. Not choosing the stretch option would have cost nearly $800,000 and had impacts on six of Mr. Cleaver's loved ones.*

Unfortunately, many things may also play a role in failing to stretch IRA distributions. It can be tempting for a beneficiary to take a lump sum of money despite the tax consequences. Fortunately, if you want to solidify your plan for distribution, there are options that will allow you to open up an IRA and incorporate "spendthrift" clauses for your beneficiaries. This will ensure your legacy is stretched appropriately and to your specifications. Only certain insurance companies allow this option, and you will not find this benefit with any brokerage accounts. You need to work with a financial professional who has the appropriate relationship with an insurance company that provides this option.

## CHAPTER 13 RECAP //

- Your legacy encompasses more than just the dollars and cents you leave for your family; it's how you want to be remembered.

- If you don't plan for your legacy, then it will be planned for you. The money that you do not use during your lifetime will either go to loved ones, unloved ones, charity, or the IRS. The question is, who would you rather disinherit?

- With a traditional IRA, your beneficiaries may inherit your tax burden depending on where that money came from.

- Failing to maximize your legacy can cost your beneficiaries thousands of dollars. With the counsel of a financial professional, it's possible to structure your assets in ways that maximize distributions to your beneficiaries. For best results, the plan must be made before you pass away.

- Stretch IRAs give beneficiaries the option of taking smaller distributions over the course of their lifetime, which allows them to take advantage of interest compounded over several years.

- Legacy planning begins with a simple list.

- A financial professional can help review the details of the assets you have designated to be a part of your legacy and make sure that you aren't unintentionally disinheriting your heirs.

# 14

# ESTATE PLANNING
# VEHICLES

*"There are some people who watch NASCAR for the highly skilled*
*driving—but most people watch it for the crashes."*
– John Oliver

*Will and Jen organized their assets five years before they retired. As a*
*retired radiologist and real estate agent, they had done very well for*
*themselves and managed to accumulate a sizeable IRA and 401(k).*
*With a combination of IRA to Roth IRA conversions, a series of*
*income annuities and a well-planned money management strategy*
*overseen by their financial professional, Will and Jen easily filled their*
*income gap and were set up to enjoy retired life. They were concerned,*
*however, about how to transfer their estate on to their two sons.*

*Will and Jen had two concerns: first, they wanted to keep as much*
*of the money in the family as possible. They didn't want their estate*

eaten up with court costs. Secondly, they were concerned about leaving a lump sum of money to their youngest son, Max. While he was a talented musician, Max had gotten involved with the wrong crowd. A serious and prolonged drug addiction had managed to destroy the music career he had always dreamed of, and now he was working in a record store, trying to stay clean and get a new band together. Their oldest son, Landon, was a hardworking husband and father with a daughter who had autism. Landon was concerned about funding a long-term care situation for her once she became an adult. Will and Jen planned to leave him a large inheritance, but they worried about leaving Max an equally large sum of money. They wanted to be fair to both of their sons, but they also wanted to be smart about how the money was managed.

Will and Jen met with an attorney to draw up a will, but they quickly learned that while having a will was a good plan, it wasn't the most efficient way to distribute their legacy. In fact, relying solely on a will would create several roadblocks and do nothing to address their concerns over how the estate was distributed.

With the guidance of their financial professional, Will and Jen elected to set up a Living Trust. This gave them more control over how their assets were distributed, and it also addressed several other issues they had overlooked. They designated an executor of the estate and divided the inheritance money between the two brothers. Landon would receive his money in a lump sum, while Max would receive his as an annual payment over the course of his lifetime. They stipulated in the trust that Max would only receive the payment if he passed two random drug tests to be performed annually. If he didn't pass the drug tests, he would have to go through rehab again for a minimum of six months before the payments would resume. This ensured that both brothers received an equal share of the money tailored to their individual situations. A Living Trust was able to accomplish all their goals and more, while avoiding the nightmare of probate and unintentional disinheritance.

After spending a lifetime building your wealth, the last thing you want is to see it all crash and burn due to poor management, government fees and court costs. The news is full of stories about wealthy men and women who worked hard to build an empire, only to have it crumble and fall a few years after they passed away. This happens when there is no plan in place and family members can't agree on how best to distribute the funds, the business or real estate property. It can also happen if the estate passes through probate.

A will has the power to establish guardianship in situations where a parent passes away, but even with a will, the process of probate is usually mandatory. Even if you have your IRA structured properly as we talked about in the previous chapter, problems can and do arise with your other assets. You want your estate planning vehicles to match your specific situation. Additionally, if your estate is entirely distributed via your will, the money that your family may need to cover the costs of your medical bills, funeral expenses and estate taxes will be tied up in probate, which can last up to a year or more. While immediate family members may have the option of requesting immediate cash from your assets during probate to cover immediate health care expenses, taxes, and fees, that process comes with its own set of complications. Choosing alternative methods for distributing your legacy can make life easier for your loved ones and can help them claim more of your estate in a more timely fashion than traditional methods.

*A simpler and less tedious approach is to avoid probate altogether by structuring your estate to be distributed outside of the probate process.* The three common ways of doing this are by structuring your assets inside a life insurance plan, using individual retirement planning tools like IRAs that give you the option of designating a beneficiary upon your death, or, more comprehensively, establishing a living trust.

## THE ABRAMS TANK OF ESTATE PLANNING: A LIVING TRUST

Probate. Just speaking the word out loud can cause shivers to run down your spine. Probate's ugly reputation is well deserved. It can be a costly, time consuming process that diminishes your estate and can delay the distribution of your estate to your loved ones. Nasty stuff, by any measure. Unless you have made a clear estate plan and discussed options for avoiding probate, it is highly likely that you have many assets that might pass through probate needlessly.

*If your will and beneficiary designations aren't correctly structured, some of these assets will go through the probate process, which can turn dollars into cents.*

Probate court was designed years ago because it used to be that after people died, the assets would get raided. Probate court made sure that the assets changed ownership properly. When you own property, things can get tricky because of the process needed in order to transfer the title of ownership. This process costs money and takes time. First, they have to see if there is an encumbrance on the property, if there is money owed to the bank and any unpaid estate taxes due. All of that has to be settled before ownership changes.

Every state has a different probate process. In the state of California, the average probate process takes one year, and during that time, your beneficiaries and family members can't sell or liquidate any assets. If they do, they create additional attorney fees. For this reason, and because of the sometimes exorbitant fees that may be charged by lawyers and accountants during the process, probate has earned a nasty reputation. It is also a public event. Because the probate process happens in court, the assets you own that go through a probate procedure become part of the public record. While this may not seem like a big deal to some, other people don't want that kind of intimate information available to the public.

A living trust avoids all of this by setting everything up ahead of time. It is like an Abrams tank that can roll right on through the probate process and deliver victory to your beneficiaries as specified by you. A living trust basically takes you through the transferring process now, while you are alive, and your estate pays all of the costs up front. Any property or real estate is taken out of your name and put into the trust. As illustrated by Will and Jen's situation, you have complete control over the terms and conditions set forth in the trust. Everything is notarized and witnessed and signed by you, and as such, everything passes on to your beneficiaries without probate.

But there's more.

A living trust is a mighty and powerful vehicle. It also takes care of your financial power of attorney and your health care directive.

» *On February 25, 1990, Terri Schiavo collapsed in her St. Petersburg home after a full cardiac arrest. Due to the lack of oxygen flow to her brain, she suffered massive brain damage, and after two and a half months in a coma, her diagnosis was declared as a persistent vegetative state.*

*Her husband, Michael Schiavo, worked with Terry's doctors for eight years attempting speech and physical therapy. After eight years of no change, Michael petitioned the Sixth Circuit Court of Florida in Pinellas County, asking to remove her feeding tube pursuant to Florida Statutes Section 765.401(3). Terri's parents opposed the petition, arguing that she was still conscious. The state court determined that Terri would not wish to continue life-prolonging measures, and on April 24, 2001, her feeding tube was removed—for the first time. It was reinserted several days later, and the battle continued, moving through federal court and garnering the attention of President George Bush, who signed legislation designed to keep her alive. In all, the Schiavo case involved 14 appeals and numerous motions, petitions and hearings in the Florida courts; five suits in federal district court and four denials of certiorari from the Supreme Court of the United States.*

*On March 18, 2005, 15 years after Terri's vegetative state diagnosis, the staff at the Pinellas Park hospice facility where Terri was being cared for disconnected the feeding tube. Terri died on March 31, 2005, 15 years after her original diagnosis.*

The Terri Schiavo case attracted a great deal of attention and criticism, and both her husband and family have written books about their experiences. Regardless of your personal beliefs, the salient point here is that had Terri's wishes been recorded in writing, all of the court battles, legal costs and grief could have been prevented. This story points clearly to why it's so vitally important that you have estate planning vehicles in place so that after you are gone, things happen the way in which *you* want them to happen.

A health care directive protects your health care intentions should you become physically unable to communicate what you want. First, you spell out what treatments you want or don't want should you become terminally ill or unconscious. Second, you name someone as your health care stand-in, giving them medical power of attorney to make medical decisions on your behalf. This is not just for end of life situations, but covers incidents where all factors must be weighed and a medical decision made on your behalf. The person you appoint will have the authority to uphold your wishes.

Financial power of attorney is like the financial equivalent of a health care power of attorney. You name someone who is able to make financial decisions on your behalf should you be unable to do so. This document can save your family thousands in legal fees and court costs and you have control over what responsibilities your proxy can and cannot assume.

A living trust is one document that can cover all your needs. It insulates your estate from probate costs, establishes your health care directive and financial power of attorney. The problems it solves are avoidable if you take the time now to set yourself up in the right vehicle. In fact, you might say that failing to do estate planning is like getting into a racecar and competing against fifty other drivers on a high-speed track without wearing a helmet, a fire suit or a seatbelt. Racing that way would just be stupid. Putting on a helmet, investing in a fire suit and buckling your seat belt are simple things to do. Setting up a Living Trust is also just as simple, and the impact of having one in place just as dramatic. Establishing a Living Trust allows you to make sure your assets go where they are supposed to go, while insulating them from the hell-fire of probate court and probate attorneys who can suck the money right out of your estate.

## UNINTENTIONALLY DISINHERITING YOUR FAMILY

You would never want to unintentionally disinherit a loved one or loved ones because of confusion surrounding your legacy plan. Unfortunately, it happens. Why? This terrible situation is typically caused by a simple lack of understanding. In particular, mistakes regarding legacy distribution occur with regards to those whom people care for the most: their grandchildren.

One of the most important ways to plan for the inheritance of your grandchildren is by properly structuring the distribution of your legacy. Specifically, you need to know if your legacy is going to be distributed *per stirpes* or *per capita*.

**Per Stirpes.** *Per stirpes* is a legal term in Latin that means "by the branch." Your estate will be distributed *per stirpes* if you designate each branch of your family to receive an equal share of your estate.

In the event that your children predecease you, their share will be distributed evenly between their children—your grandchildren.

**Per Capita.** *Per capita* distribution is different in that you may designate different amounts of your estate to be distributed to members of the same generation.

Per stirpes distribution of assets will follow the family tree down the line as the predecessor beneficiaries pass away. On the other hand, per capita distribution of assets ends on the branch of the family tree with the death of a designated beneficiary. For example, when your child passes away, in a per capita distribution, your grandchildren would not receive distributions from the assets that you designated to your child.

What the terms mean is not nearly as important as what they do, however. The reality is that improperly titled assets could accidentally leave your grandchildren disinherited upon the death of their parents. It's easy to check, and it's even easier to fix.

A simple way to remember the difference between the two types of distribution goes something like this: "***Stirpes are forever and Capita is capped.***"

Another way to avoid complicated legacy distribution problems, and the probate process, is by leveraging a life insurance plan.

## LIFE INSURANCE: AN IMPORTANT LEGACY TOOL

One of the most powerful legacy tools you can leverage is a good life insurance policy. Life insurance is a highly efficient legacy tool because it creates money when it is needed or desired the most. Over the years, life insurance has become less expensive, while it offers more features, and it provides longer guarantees.

There are many unique benefits of life insurance that can help your beneficiaries get the most out of your legacy. Some of them include:

- Providing beneficiaries with a tax-free, liquid asset.

- Covering the costs associated with your death.
- Providing income for your dependents.
- Offering an investment opportunity for your beneficiaries.
- Covering expenses such as tuition or mortgage down payments for your children or grandchildren.

Very few people want life insurance, but nearly everyone wants what it does. Life insurance is specifically, and uniquely, capable of creating money when it is needed most. When a loved one passes, no amount of money can remove the pain of loss. And certainly, money doesn't solve the challenges that might arise with losing someone important.

It has been said that when you have money, you have options. When you don't have money, your options are severely limited. You might imagine a life insurance policy can give your family and loved ones options that would otherwise be impossible.

> » Ben spent the last 20 years building a small business. In so many ways, it is a family business. Each of his three children, Maddie, Ruby and Edward, worked in the shop part-time during high school. But after all three attended college, only Maddie returned to join her father, and eventually will run the business full-time when Ben retires.
>
> Ben is able to retire comfortably on Social Security and on-going income from the shop, but the business is nearly his entire financial legacy. It is his wish that Maddie own the business outright, but he also wants to leave an equal legacy to each of his three children.
>
> There is no simple way to divide the business into thirds and still leave the business intact for Maddie.
>
> Ben ends up buying a life insurance policy to make up the difference. Ruby and Edward will receive their share of an

*inheritance in cash from the life insurance policy and Maddie*
*will be able to inherit the business intact.*

*Ben is able to accomplish his goals, treat all three children*
*equitably and leave Maddie the business she helped to build.*

If you have a life insurance policy but you haven't looked at it in a while, you may not know how it operates, how much it is worth and how it will be distributed to your beneficiaries. You may also need to update your beneficiaries on your policy. In short, without a comprehensive review of your policy, you don't really know where the money will go or to whom it will go.

If you don't have a life insurance policy but are looking for options to maintain and grow your legacy, speaking with a professional can show you the benefits of life insurance. Many people don't consider buying a life insurance policy until some event in their life triggers it, like the loss of a loved one, an accident or a health condition.

## BENEFITS OF LIFE INSURANCE

Life insurance is a useful and secure tool for contingency planning, ensuring that your dependents receive the assets that you want them to have, and for meeting the financial goals you have set for the future. While it bears the name "Life Insurance," it is, in reality, a diverse financial tool that can meet many needs. The main function of a life insurance policy is to provide financial assets for your survivors. Life insurance is particularly efficient at achieving this goal because it provides a tax-advantaged lump sum of money in the form of a death benefit to your beneficiary or beneficiaries. That financial asset can be used in a number of ways. It can be structured as an investment to provide income for your spouse or children, it can pay down debts, and it can be used to cover estate taxes and other costs associated with death.

Tax liabilities on the estate you leave behind are inevitable. Capital property, for instance, is taxed at its fair market value at the time of your death, unless that property is transferred to your spouse. If the property has appreciated during the time you owned it, taxation on capital gains will occur. Registered Retirement Savings Plans (RRSPs) and other similarly structured assets are also included as taxable income unless transferred to a beneficiary as well. Those are just a few examples of how an estate can become subject to a heavy tax burden. The unique benefits of a life insurance policy provide ways to handle this tax burden, solving any liquidity problems that may arise if your family members want to hold onto an illiquid asset, such as a piece of property or an investment. Life insurance can provide a significant amount of money to a family member or other beneficiary, and that money is likely to remain exempt from taxation or seizure.

One of life insurance's most important benefits is that it is not considered part of the estate of the policy holder. The death benefit that is paid by the insurance company goes exclusively to the beneficiaries listed on the policy. This shields the proceeds of the policy from fees and costs that can reduce an estate, including probate proceedings, attorneys' fees and claims made by creditors. The distribution of your life insurance policy is also unaffected by delays of the estate's distribution, like probate. Your beneficiaries will get the proceeds of the policy in a timely fashion, regardless of how long it takes for the rest of your estate to be settled.

Investing a portion of your assets in a life insurance policy can also protect that portion of your estate from creditors. If you owe money to someone or some entity at the time of your death, a creditor is not able to claim any money from a life insurance policy or an annuity, for that matter. An exception to this rule is if you had already used the life insurance policy as collateral against a loan. If a large portion of the money you want to dedicate to your legacy is sitting in a savings account, investment or other liquid form, creditors may be able to receive their claim on it before your beneficiaries get anything, that is if there's anything left. A life insurance policy protects your assets from creditors and ensures that your beneficiaries get the money that you intend them to have.

## HOW MUCH LIFE INSURANCE DO YOU NEED?

Determining the type of policy and the amount right for you depends on an analysis of your needs. A financial professional can help you complete a needs analysis that will highlight the amount of insurance that you require to meet your goals. This type of personalized review will allow you to determine ways to continue providing income for your spouse or any dependents you may have. A financial professional can also help you calculate the amount of income that your policy should replace to meet the needs of your beneficiaries and the duration of the distribution of that income.

You may also want to use your life insurance policy to meet any expenses associated with your death. These can include funeral costs, fees from probate and legal proceedings, and taxes. You may also want to dedicate a portion of your policy proceeds to help fund tuition or other expenses for your children or grandchildren. You can buy a policy and hope it covers all of those costs, or you can work with a professional who can calculate exactly how much insurance you need and how to structure it to meet your goals. Which would you rather do?

## AVOIDING POTENTIAL SNAGS

There are benefits to having life insurance supersede the direction given in a will or other estate plan, but there are also some potential snags that you should address to meet your wishes. For example, if your will instructs that your assets be divided equally between your two children but your life insurance beneficiary is listed as just one of the children, the assets in the life insurance policy will only be distributed to the child listed as the beneficiary. The beneficiary designation of your life insurance supersedes your will's instruction. This is important to understand when designating beneficiaries on a policy you purchase. Work with a professional to make sure that your beneficiaries are accurately listed on your assets, especially your life insurance policies.

## USING LIFE INSURANCE TO BUILD YOUR LEGACY

Depending on your goals, there are strategies you can use that could multiply how much you leave behind. Life insurance is one of the most surefire and efficient investment tools for building a substantial legacy that will meet your financial goals.

Here is a brief overview of how life insurance can boost your legacy:

- Life insurance provides an immediate increase in your legacy.
- It provides an income tax-advantaged death benefit for your beneficiaries.
- A good life insurance policy has the opportunity to accumulate value over time.
- It may have an option to include long-term care (LTC) or chronic illness benefits should you require them.

If your Green Money income needs for retirement are met and you have Yellow Money assets that will provide for your future expenses, you may have extra assets that you want to earmark as legacy funds. By electing to invest those assets into a life insurance policy, you can immediately increase the amount of your legacy. Remember, **life insurance allows you to transfer a tax-advantaged lump sum of money to your beneficiaries. It remains in your control during your lifetime, can provide for your long-term care needs and bypasses probate costs.** And make no mistake, taxes can have a huge impact on your legacy. Not only that, income and assets from your legacy can have tax implications for your beneficiaries, as well.

Here's a brief overview of how taxes could affect your legacy and your beneficiaries:

- The higher your income, the higher the rate at which it is taxed.
- Withdrawals from qualified plans are taxed as income.
- What's more, when you leave a large qualified plan, it ends up being taxed at a high rate.
- If you left a $500,000 IRA to your child, they could end up owing as much as $140,000 in income taxes.
- However, if you could just withdraw $50,000 a year, the tax bill might only be $10,000 per year.

How could you use that annual amount to leave a larger legacy? Luckily, you can leverage a life insurance policy to avoid those tax penalties, preserving a larger amount of your legacy and freeing your beneficiaries from an added tax burden.

> » When Brenda turned 70 years old, she decided it was time to look into life insurance policy options. She still feels young, but she remembers that her mother died in early 70s, and she wants to plan ahead so she can pass on some of her legacy to her grandchildren just like her grandmother did for her.
>
> Brenda doesn't really want to think about life insurance, but she does want the security, reliability and tax-advantaged distribution that it offers. She lives modestly, and her Social Security benefit meets most of her income needs. As the beneficiary of her late husband's Certificate of Deposit (CD), she has $100,000 in an account that she has never used and doesn't anticipate ever needing since her income needs were already met.

*After looking at several different investment options with a professional, Brenda decides that a Single Premium life insurance policy fits her needs best. She can buy the policy with a $100,000 one-time payment and she is guaranteed that it would provide more than the value of the contract to her beneficiaries. If she left the money in the CD, it would be subject to taxes. But for every dollar that she puts into the life insurance policy, her beneficiaries are guaranteed at least that dollar plus a death benefit, and all of it will be **tax-free!***

*For $100,000, Brenda's particular policy offers a $170,000 death benefit distribution to her beneficiaries. By moving the $100,000 from a CD to a life insurance policy, Brenda increases her legacy by 70 percent. Not only that, she has also sheltered it from taxes, so her beneficiaries will be able to receive $1.70 for every $1.00 that she entered into the policy! While buying the policy doesn't allow her to use the money for herself, it does allow her family to benefit from her well-planned legacy.*

## MAKE YOUR WISHES KNOWN

Estate taxes used to be a much hotter topic in the mid-2000s when the estate tax limits and exclusions were much smaller and taxed at a higher rate than today. In 2008, estates valued at $2 million or more were taxed at 45 percent. Just two years later, the limit was raised to $5 million dollars taxed at 35 percent. The limit has continued to rise ever since. The limit applies to fewer people than before. Estate organization, however, is just as important as ever, and it affects everyone.

Ask yourself:

- Are your assets actually titled and held the way you think they are?
- Are your beneficiaries set up the way you think they should be?

- Have there been changes to your family or those you desire as beneficiaries?

There is more to your legacy beyond your property, money, investments and other assets that you leave to family members, loved ones and charities. Everyone has a legacy beyond money. You also leave behind personal items of importance, your values and beliefs, your personal and family history, and your wishes. Beyond a will and a plan for your assets, it is important that you make your wishes known to someone for the rest of your personal legacy. When it comes time for your family and loved ones to make decisions after you are gone, knowing your wishes can help them make decisions that honor you and your legacy, and give meaning to what you leave behind. Your professional can help you organize.

Think about your:
- Personal stories / recollections
- Values
- Personal items of emotional significance
- Financial assets

Do you want to make a plan to pass these things on to your family?

## WORKING WITH A PROFESSIONAL

Part of using life insurance to your greatest advantage is selecting the policy and provider that can best meet your goals. Venturing into the jungle of policies, brokers and salespeople can be overwhelming, and can leave you wondering if you've made the best decision. Working with a trusted financial professional can help you cut through the red tape, the "sales-speak" and confusion to find a policy that meets your goals and best serves your desires for your money. If you already have a policy, a financial professional can help you review it and become familiar with the policy's premium, the guarantees the policy affords, its performance, and its features and benefits. A financial professional can also help you make any necessary changes to the policy.

> » *When Cheryl turned 88, her daughter finally convinced her to meet with a financial professional to help her organize her assets and get her legacy in order. Although Cheryl is reluctant to let a stranger in on her personal finances, she ends up very glad that she did.*
>
> *In the process of listing Cheryl's assets and her beneficiaries, her professional finds a man's name listed as the beneficiary of an old life insurance annuity that she owns. It turns out, the man is Cheryl's ex-husband who is still alive. Had Cheryl passed away before her ex-husband, the annuities and any death benefits that came with them, would have been passed on to her ex-husband. This does not reflect her latest wishes.*

Things change, relationships evolve and the way you would like your legacy organized needs to adapt to the changes that happen throughout your life. There may be a new child or grandchild in your family, or you may have been divorced or remarried. A professional will regularly review your legacy assets and ask you questions to make sure that everything is up to date and that the current organization reflects your current wishes.

## CHAPTER 14 RECAP //

- A Living Trust is a mighty vehicle when it comes to the proper transfer of your estate. It avoids the nightmare of probate, provides for a financial power of attorney and health care directive. It also allows you to specify the terms and conditions of the inheritance so that your assets are passed on in the manner that you wish.

- To avoid unintentional disinheritance, understand the difference between the designations *per stirpes* and *per capita*.

- Most people don't want life insurance, but they do want what it does. Life insurance has the ability to create a liquid, tax-free lump sum of money that pays out significantly more than what was paid into it. As a legacy tool, it allows you to leverage more of your money with less capital.

- Life insurance provides for the distribution of tax-free, liquid assets to your beneficiaries and can significantly build your legacy. They can also provide Living Benefits to help you pay for the high costs of medical care while you are still living.

- Working with a financial professional can help you select the policy that best meets your needs, or can help you fine tune your existing policy to better reflect your desires and intentions.

# 15

# WHO'S GOT YOUR BACK?
## CHOOSING A PROFESSIONAL YOU TRUST

*"I watched him strap on his harness and helmet, climb into the cockpit and, minutes later, a black dot falls off the wing two thousand feet above our field. At almost the same instant, a white streak behind him flowered out into the delicate wavering muslin of a parachute—a few gossamer yards grasping onto air and suspending below them, with invisible threads, a human life, a man who by stitches, cloth, and cord, had made himself a god of the sky for those immortal moments."*
– Charles Lindbergh

From the moment you step up into your retirement vehicle with all your gear in tow, your assets organized, your income needs met, and your accumulation and legacy plans in place, working with a professional that you trust can make all the difference in how well your retirement reflects your desires.

It is important to know what you are looking for before hitting the accelerator or taking the jump. There are many people that would love to handle your money, but not everyone is qualified to handle it in a way that leads to a holistic approach to creating a solid retirement plan. Here's the thing to remember: *No one will ever care more about your money than you do.*

## YOUR TANDEM MASTER

In skydiving, the newly initiated can experience the thrill of being "a god in the sky" with the help of a trained professional, known as a Tandem Instructor. So it follows, if retiring is like jumping out of an airplane into the space of the great unknown, you have to ask yourself, who do you want to be strapped to? It's not overly dramatic to say that you are putting your life into the hands of the financial professional you choose to trust with your life's savings. The distinction being made here is that you should look for someone that puts your interests first and actively wants to help you meet your goals and objectives. Oftentimes, the products someone sells you matter less than their dedication to making sure that you have a plan that meets your needs.

Professionals held to fiduciary standards of liability take your whole financial position into consideration. They make plans that adjust your risk exposure, invest in tools that secure your desired income during retirement and create investment strategies that allow you to continue accumulating wealth during your retirement for you to use later or to contribute to your legacy. If you buy stocks with a broker, use a different agent for a life insurance policy and have an unmanaged 401(k) through your employer, working with a financial professional will consolidate the management of your assets so you have one trustworthy person quarterbacking all of the team elements of your portfolio.

Financial products and investment tools change, but the concepts that lie behind wise retirement planning are lasting. In the end, a financial professional's approach is designed for those serious about planning for retirement. *Can you say the same thing about the person that advises you about your financial life?*

It's easy to see how choosing a financial professional can be one of the most important decisions you can make in your life. Not only do they provide you with advice, they also manage the personal assets that supply your retirement income and contribute to your legacy. So, how do you find a good one?

## HOW TO FIND A FINANCIAL PROFESSIONAL YOU CAN TRUST

Taking care to select a financial professional is one of the best things you can do for yourself and for your future. Your professional has influence and control of your investment decisions, making their role in your life more than just important. Your financial security and the quality of your retirement depends on the decisions, investment strategies and asset structuring that you and your professional create.

Working with a professional is different than calling up a broker when you want to buy or trade some stock. This isn't a decision that you can hand off to anyone else. You need to bring your time and attention to the table when it comes to finding someone with whom you can entrust your financial life. Separating the wheat from the chaff will take some work, but you'll be happy you did it.

While no one can tell you exactly who to choose or how to choose them, the following information can help you narrow the field:

- You can start by asking your friends, family and colleagues for referrals. You will want to pay particular attention to the recommendations that you get from others who are in your similar financial situation and who have similar lifestyle choices. The professional for the CEO of your company may have a different skill-set than the skill-set of the professional befitting your cousin who has three kids and a Subaru like you. Do follow-up research on the Internet as well. Look up the people who have been recommended to you on websites like LinkedIn that show the work history, referrals and experience of the candidates that you find most attractive. You will also learn about the firms with or for whom they work. The investment philosophies and reputations of the companies they work for will tell you a lot about how they will handle your money.

- The other side of the coin, however, is that everyone and their brother has a recommendation about how you should manage your money and who should manage it for you. From hot stock tips to "the best money manager in the state," people love to share good information that makes them look like they are in-the-know. Nobody wants to talk about the bad stock purchases they made, the times they lost money and the poor selections they made regarding financial professionals or stock brokers. If you decide to take a friend or family member's recommendation, make sure they have a substantial, long-term experience with the financial professional and that their glowing review isn't just based on a one-time "win."

- You can also use online tools like the search function of the Financial Planning Association (http://www.fpanet. org/) and the National Association of Personal Financial professionals (http://www.napfa.org/). Most of the professionals listed on these sites do not earn commissions from selling financial products, but are instead paid on a fee-only basis for their services. It is important to understand how your professional is being paid. It is generally considered preferable to work with a fee-based professional who will not have conflicts of interests between earning a commission and acting in your best interests.

• Many professionals may also be brokers or dealers that can earn commissions on things like life insurance, certain types of annuities and disability insurance. These professionals have most likely intentionally overlapped their roles so that if their clients choose to purchase insurance or investment products that require a broker or dealer, those clients won't have to find an additional person to work with. Again, understanding the role of your professional will help you make your determination.

## NARROWING THE FIELD

**1. Decide on the Type of Professional with Whom You Want to Work.** There are four basic kinds of financial professionals. Many professionals may play overlapping roles. It is important to know a professional's primary function, how they charge for their services and whether they are obligated to act in your best interest.

*Registered representatives*, better known as stockbrokers or bank / investment representatives, make their living by earning commissions on insurance products and investment services. Stockbrokers basically sell you things. The products from which they make the highest commission are sometimes the products that they recommend to their clients. If you want to make a simple transaction, such as buying or selling a particular stock, a registered representative can help you. Although registered representatives are licensed professionals, if you want to create a structured and planful approach to positioning your assets for retirement, you might want to consider continuing your search.

The term "planner" is often misused. It can refer to credible professionals that are CPAs, CFPs and ChFCs to your uncle's next door neighbor who claims to have a lead on some undervalued stock about to be "discovered." A wide array of people may claim to be planners because there are no requirements to be a planner. The term financial planner, however, refers to someone who is properly registered as an investment advisor and serves as a fiduciary as described below.

Financial professionals are the diamonds in the rough. These Registered Investment Advisors are compensated on a fee basis. They do, however, often have licensure as stockbrokers or insurance agents, allowing them to earn commissions on certain transactions. More importantly, **financial professionals are financial fiduciaries, meaning they are required to make financial decisions in your best interest and reflecting your risk tolerance.** Investment Advisors are held to high ethical standards and are highly regarded in the financial industry. Financial professionals also often take a more comprehensive approach to asset management. These professionals are trained and credentialed to plan and coordinate their clients' assets in order to meet their goals or retirement and legacy planning. They are not focused on individual stocks, investments or markets. They look at the big picture, the whole enchilada.

*Money managers* are on par with financial professionals. However, they are often given explicit permission to make investment decisions without advanced approval by their clients.

Understanding who you are working with and what their title is the first step to planning your retirement. While each of the above-mentioned types of financial professionals can help you with aspects of your finances, it is financial professionals who have the most intimate role, the most objective investment strategies and the most unbiased mode of compensation for their services. A financial professional can also help you with the non-financial aspects of your legacy and can help you find ways to create a tax planning strategy to help you save money.

**2. Be Objective.** At the end of the day, you need to separate the weak from the strong. While you might want a strong personal rapport with your professional, or you may want to choose your professional for their personality and positive attitude, it is more important that you find someone who will give sage advice regarding achieving your retirement goals.

It can be helpful to use a process of elimination to narrow the field of potential professionals. Look into five or six potential leads and cross off your list the ones that don't meet your requirements until only one or two remain. Cross-check your remaining choices against the list of things you need from a professional. Make sure they represent a firm that has the investment tools and products that you desire, and make sure they have experience in retirement planning. That is, after all, the main goal.

Don't be afraid to investigate each of your candidates. You'll want to ask the same questions and look for the same information from everyone you consider so you can then compare them and discern which is best for you. You'll want to take a look at the specific credentials of each professional, their experience and competence, their ethics and fiduciary status, their history and track record, and a list of the services that they offer. The professionals who meet all or most of your qualifications are the ones you will contact for an interview.

Potential professionals should meet your qualifications in the following categories:

- *Credentials:* Look at their experience, the quality of their education, any associations to which they belong and certifications they have earned. Someone who has continued their professional education through ongoing certifications will be more up-to-date on current financial practices compared to someone who got their degree 25 years ago and hasn't done a thing since.

- *Practices:* Look at the track record of your candidates, how they are compensated for their services, the reports and analysis they offer, and their value added services.
- *Services:* Your professional must meet your needs. If you are planning your retirement, you should work with someone who offers services that help you to that end. You want someone who can offer planning, advice on investment strategies, ways to calculate risk, advice on insurance and annuities products, and ways to manage your tax strategy.
- *Ethics:* You want to work with someone who is above board and does things the right way. Vet them by checking their compliance record, current licensing, fiduciary status and, yes, even their criminal record. You never know!

**3. Ask for and Check References.** Once you have selected two or three professionals that you want to meet, call or email them and ask for references. Every professional should be able to provide you with at least two or three names. In fact, they will probably be eager to share them with you. Most professionals rely on references for validation of their success, quality of services and likability. You should, however, take them with a grain of salt. You have no way to know whether or not references are a professional's friends or colleagues.

It is worth contacting references, however, to check for inconsistencies. Ask each reference the same set of questions to get the same basic information. How long have they been working with the professional? What kind of services have they used and were they happy with them? What type of financial planning did they use the professional for? Were they versed in the type of financial planning that you needed? You can also ask them direct questions to elicit candid responses. What was the full cost of the expenses that your professional charged you? Do the reports and statements you receive come from the same firm? Questions like these can help you get a sense of how well the reference knows their professional and whether or not they are a quality reference. A good reference is a bit like icing on the cake. It's nice to have them, but nothing speaks louder than a good track record and quality experience. And remember that a good reference, while nice to hear, is relatively cheap. How many times have you heard someone on the golf course or at work telling you how great their stockbroker is? But how many times have you heard about the bad investments or losses they have experienced?

**4. Use the Internet.** As a final step before picking up the phone and calling your candidates, do some digging to discover if anyone on your list has a history of unlawful or unethical practices, or has been disciplined for any of their professional behavior or decisions. Don't worry, you don't have to hire a private investigator. You can easily find this information on the Financial Industry Regulatory Authority's (FINRA) online BrokerCheck tool: http://www.finra.org/Investors/ToolsCalculators/BrokerCheck/.

You should obviously explore the website of a potential professional and the website of the firm that they represent. The internet allows you to go beyond the online business card of a professional to gain access to information that they don't control. It may all be good information! Or a brief search of the internet could reveal a sketchy past. The best part is that the internet allows you to find helpful information in an anonymous fashion.

Start with Google (www.google.com) and search the name of a potential professional and their firm. Keep your eyes trained on third party sources such as articles, blog posts or news stories that mention the professional. You can also check a professional's compliance records online with the Financial Industry Regulatory Authority (FINRA) and the Securities and Exchange Commission (SEC). If you want to dig deeper, you can combine search terms like "scams," "lawsuits," "suspensions" and "fraud" with a professional's or firm's name to see what information arises. More likely than not, you won't find anything. But if you do, you'll be glad that you checked.

## HOW TO INTERVIEW CANDIDATES

After vetting your candidates and narrowing down a list of professionals that you think might be a good fit for you, it's time to start interviewing.

When you meet in person with a professional, you want to take advantage of your time with them. The presentations and information that they share with you will be important to pay attention to, but you will also want to control some aspects of the interview. After a professional has told you what they want you to hear, it's time to ask your own questions to get the specific information you need to make your decision.

Make sure to prepare a list of questions and an informal agenda so that you can keep track of what you want to ask and what points you want the professional to touch on during the interview. Using the same questions and agenda will also allow you to more easily compare the professionals after you have interviewed them all. Remember that these interviews are just that, *interviews*. You are meeting with several professionals to determine with whom you want to work. Don't agree to anything or sign anything during an interview until after you have made your final decision.

It can also be helpful to put a time limit on your interviews and to meet the professionals at their offices. The time limit will keep things on track and will allow structured time for presentations and questions/discussion. By meeting them at their office, you can get a sense of the work environment, the staff culture and attitude, and how the firm does business. If you are unable to travel to a professional's office and must meet them at your home or office, make sure that your interviews are scheduled with plenty of time between so the professionals don't cross each other's paths.

You can use the following questions during an initial interview to get an understanding of how each professional does business and whether they are a good fit for you:

**1. How do you charge for your services? How much do you charge?** This information should be easy to find on their website, but if you don't see it, ask. Find out if they charge an initial planning fee, if they charge a percentage for assets under their management and if they make money by selling specific financial products or services. If so, you should follow up by asking how much the service costs. This will give you an idea of how they really make their money and if they have incentive to sell certain products over others. Make sure you understand exactly how you will be charged so there are no surprises down the road if you decide to work with this person.

**2. What are your credentials, licenses, and certifications?** There are Certified Financial Planners (CFPs), Chartered Financial Consultants (ChFCs), Investment Advisor Representatives, Certified Public Accountants (CPAs) and Personal Financial Specialists (PFSs). Whatever their credentials or titles, you want to be sure that the professional you work with is an expert in the field relevant to your circumstances. If you want someone to manage your money, you will most likely look for an Investment Advisor. Someone that works with an independent firm will likely have a team of CPAs, CFPs and other financial experts upon whom they can draw. If you like the professional you are meeting with and you think they might be a good fit, but they don't have the accounting experience you want them to have, ask about their firm and the resources available to them. If they work closely with CPAs that are experienced in your needs, it could be a good match.

**3. What are the financial services that you and your firm provide?** The question within the question here is, "Can you help me achieve my goals?" Some people can only provide you with investment advice, and others are tax consultants. You will likely want to work with someone that provides a complete suite of financial planning services and products that touch on retirement planning, insurance options, legacy and estate structuring, and tax planning. Whatever services they provide, make sure they meet your needs and your anticipated needs.

**4. What kinds of clients do you work with the most?** A lot of financial professionals work within a niche: retirement planning, risk assessment, life insurance, etc. Finding someone who works with other people that are in the same financial boat as you and who have similar goals can be an important way to make sure they understand your needs. While someone might be a crackerjack annuities cowboy, you might not be interested in that option. Ask follow-up questions that will really help you understand where their expertise lies and whether or not their experience lines up with your needs.

**5. May I see a sample of one of your financial plans?** You wouldn't buy a car without test driving it, and you should not work with a professional without seeing a sample of how they do business. While there is no formal structure that a financial plan has to follow, the variation between professionals can help you find someone who "speaks your language." One professional may provide you with an in-depth analysis that relies heavily on info graphics and diagrams. Someone else may give you a seven page review of your assets and general recommendations. By seeing a sample plan, you can narrow down who presents information in the way that you desire and in ways that you understand.

**6. How do you approach investing?** You may be entirely in the dark about how to approach your investments, or you might have some guiding principles. Either way, ask each candidate what their philosophy is. Some will resonate with you and some won't. A good professional who has a realistic approach to investing won't promise you the moon or tell you that they can make you a lot of money. Professionals who are successful at retirement planning and full service financial management will tell you that they will listen to your goals, risk tolerance and comfort level with different types of investment strategies. Working with someone that you trust is critical, and this question in particular can help you find out who you can and who you can't.

**7. How do you remain in contact with your clients?** Does your prospective professional hold annual, quarterly or monthly meetings? How often do *you* want to meet with your professional? Some people want to check in once a year, go over everything and make sure their ducks are all in a row. If any changes over the previous year or additions to their legacy planning strategy came up, they'll do it on that date. Other people want a monthly update to be more involved in the decision making process and to understand what's happening with their portfolio. You basically need to determine the right degree of involvement for both you and your financial professional. You'll also want to feel out how your professional communicates. Do you prefer phone calls or face-to-face meetings? Do you want your professional to explain things to you in detail or to summarize for you what decisions they've made? Is the professional willing to give you their direct phone number or their email address? More importantly, do you want that information and do you want to be able to contact them in those ways?

**8. Are you my main contact, or do you work with a team?** This is another way of finding out how involved with you your professional will be, and how often they will meet with you. It is also a way to discover how the firm they represent operates and manages their clients. Some professionals will answer their own phone, meet with you regularly and have your home phone number on speed dial. Others will meet with you once a year and have a partner or assistant check in with you every quarter to give you an update. Other companies take an entirely team-based approach whereby clients have a main contact but their portfolio is handled by a team of professionals that represent the firm. One way isn't better than another, but one way will be best for you. Find out how the professional you are interviewing operates before entering into an agreement.

**9. How do you provide a unique experience for your clients?** This is a polite way of asking, "Why should I work with you?" A professional should have a compelling answer to this question that connects with you. Their answer will likely touch on their investment philosophy, their communication style and their expertise. If you hear them describing strengths and philosophies that resonate with you, keep them on your list. Some professionals will tell you that they will make investments with your money that match your values, others will say they will maximize your returns and others will say they will protect your capital while structuring your assets for income. Whatever you're looking for in a professional, you will most likely find it in the answer to this question.

This last question you will want to ask *yourself* after you've met with someone who you are considering hiring:

**10. Did they ask questions and show signs that they were interested in working with me?** A professional who will structure your assets to reflect your risk tolerance and to position you for a comfortable retirement must be a good listener. You will want to pass by a professional who talks non-stop and tells you what to do without listening to what you want them to do. If you felt they listened well and understood your needs, and seemed interested and experienced in your situation, then they might be right for you.

## THE IMPORTANCE OF INDEPENDENCE

Not all investment firms and financial professionals are created equal. The information in this book has systematically shown that leveraging investments for income and accumulation in today's market requires new ideas and modern planning. In short, you need innovative ideas to come up with the creative solutions that will provide you with the retirement that you want. Innovation thrives on independence. No matter how good a financial professional is, the firm that they represent needs to operate on principles that make sense in today's economy. Remember, advice about money has been around forever. Good advice, however, changes with the times.

Timing the market, relying on the sale of stocks for income and banking on high treasury and bond returns are not strategies. They aren't even realistic ways to make money or to generate income. Working with an independent agent can help you break free from the old ways of thinking and position you to create a realistic retirement plan.

Working with an independent professional who relies on fee-based income tied to the success of their performance will also give you greater peace of mind. When you do well, they do well, and that's the way it should be. Your independent financial professional will make sure that:

- Your assets are organized and structured to reflect your risk tolerance.
- Your assets will be available to you when you need them and in the way that you need them.
- You will have a lifetime income that will support your lifestyle through your retirement.
- You are handling your taxes as efficiently as possible.
- Your legacy is in order.
- Your Red Money is turned into Yellow Money, and is managed in your best interest.

» *Remember Buzz and Tamara from Chapter 1? Even though they knew they had Social Security benefits coming, they placed some money in savings and each had a pension or a 401(k).* **Before they met with a financial professional, they had no idea what their retirement would look like.** *After they met with an agent, they knew exactly what types of assets they had, how much they were worth, how much risk they were exposed to and how they were going to be distributed. They also created an income plan so that they could pay their bills every month the moment they retired, and they maximized their Social Security benefit by targeting the year and month they would get the most lifetime benefits. After their income needs were met, they were able to continue accumulating wealth by investing their extra assets to serve them in the future and contribute to their legacy. Their professional also helped them make decisions that impacted their taxes, protecting the value of their assets and allowing them to keep more of their money.*

*This isn't a fairy tale scenario. This is an example of how much you stand to gain by meeting with a financial professional who can help you create a planful approach to your retirement. The concept of Know So and Hope So didn't just apply to their money, it also applied to Ryan and Amy. They* **hoped** *that they would have enough for retirement and that they had worked hard enough and saved enough to maintain their lifestyle. Working with a financial professional allowed them to* **know** *that their income needs were secured and structured to provide them with income for the rest of their lives and with some money to spare.*

*Now, ask yourself: Is your retirement built on hopes and dreams, or a solid, predictable plan?*

## IT'S WORTH IT!

Finding, interviewing and selecting a financial professional can seem like a daunting task. And honestly, it will take a good amount of work to narrow the field and find the one you want. In the end, it is worth the blood, sweat and tears. Your retirement, lifestyle, assets and legacy is on the line. The choices you make today will have lasting impacts on your life and the life of your loved ones. Working with someone you trust and know you can rely on to make decisions that will benefit you is invaluable. The work it takes to find them is something you will never regret.

Here is a recap of why working with a financial professional is the best retirement decision you can make:

## CHAPTER 15 RECAP //

- It's not overly dramatic to say that you are putting your life into the hands of the financial professional you choose to trust with your life's savings. Look for professionals held to fiduciary standards of liability who put your interests first and actively want to help you meet your goals and objectives. Your risk tolerance, needs, wants, liquidity concerns and timeline worries should be the focus of the meeting before they try to sell you any products.

- To find a professional you can trust, start by asking family and friends for referrals. Make sure to do your due diligence and check out the references of anyone who is recommended to you. Look for resources online such as the Financial Planning Association and the National Association of Personal Financial professionals.

- When interviewing candidates, make sure you understand how they charge for their services. Also look for real-time life experience, licenses and certifications. Ask questions such as, "How often do you check in with your clients?" "May I see a sample of one of your financial plans?" and, "How do you approach investing?" These questions will help ensure that you and your professional are a good fit for each other.

# GLOSSARY[*]

**ANNUAL RESET** *(ANNUAL RATCHET, CLIQUET)* – Crediting methods measuring index movement over a one year period. Positive interest is calculated and credited at the end of each contract year and cannot be lost if the index subsequently declines. Say that the index increased from 100 to 110 in one year and the indexed annuity had an 80 percent participation rate. The insurance company would take the 10 percent gross index gain for the year (110-100/100), apply the participation rate (10 percent index gain x 80 percent rate) and credit 8 percent interest to the annuity. But, what if in the following year the index declined back to 100? The individual would keep the 8 percent interest earned and simply receive zero interest for the down year. An annual reset structure

---

\* *"Glossary of Terms." FixedAnnuityFacts.com. NAFA, the National Association for Fixed Annuities, n.d. 12 Nov. 2013* preserves credited gains and treats negative index periods as years with zero growth.

**ANNUITANT** – The person, usually the annuity owner, whose life expectancy is used to calculate the income payment amount on the annuity.

**ANNUITY** – An annuity is a contract issued by an insurance company that often serves as a type of savings plan used by individuals looking for long term growth and protection of assets that will likely be needed within retirement.

**AVERAGING** – Index values may either be measured from a start point to an end point (point-to-point) or values between the start point and end point may be averaged to determine an ending value. Index values may be averaged over the days, weeks, months or quarters of the period.

**BENEFICIARY** – A beneficiary is the person designated to receive payments due upon the death of the annuity owner or the annuitant themselves.

**BONUS RATE** – A bonus rate is the "extra" or "additional" interest paid during the first year (the initial guarantee period), typically used as an added incentive to get consumers to select their annuity policy over another.

**CALL OPTION** *(ALSO SEE PUT OPTION)* – Gives the holder the right to buy an underlying security or index at a specified price on or before a given date.

**CAP** – The maximum interest rate that will be credited to the annuity for the year or period. The cap usually refers to the maximum interest credited after applying the participation rate or yield spread. If the index methodology showed a 20 percent increase, the participation rate was 60 percent and the maximum interest cap was 10 percent, the contract would credit 10 percent interest. A few annuities use a maximum gain cap instead of a maximum interest cap with the participation rate or yield spread applied to the lesser of the gain or the cap. If the index methodology showed a 20 percent increase, the participation rate was 60 percent and the maximum gain cap was 10 percent, the contract would credit 6 percent interest.

**COMPOUND INTEREST** – Interest is earned on both the original principal and on previously earned interest. It is more favorable than simple interest. Suppose that your original principal was $1 and your interest rate was 10 percent for five years. With simple interest, your value is ($1 + $0.10 interest each year) = $1.50. With compound interest, your value is ($1 x 1.10 x 1.10 x 1.10 x 1.10 x 1.10) = $1.61. The advantage of compound interest over simple interest becomes greater as each subsequent period passes.

**CREDITING METHOD** *(ALSO SEE METHODOLOGY)* – The formula(s) used to determine the excess interest that is credited above the minimum interest guarantee.

**DEATH BENEFITS** – The payment the annuity owner's estate or beneficiaries will receive if he or she dies before the annuity matures. On most annuities, this is equal to the current account value. Some annuities offer an enhanced value at death via an optional rider that has a monthly or annual fee associated with it.

**EXCESS INTEREST** – Interest credited to the annuity contract above the minimum guaranteed interest rate. In an indexed annuity the excess interest is determined by applying a stated crediting method to a specific index or indices.

**FIXED ANNUITY** – A contract issued by an insurance company guaranteeing a minimum interest rate with the crediting of excess interest determined by the performance of the insurer's general account. Index annuities are fixed annuities.

**FIXED DEFERRED ANNUITY** – With fixed annuities, an insurance company offers a guaranteed interest rate plus safety of your principal and earnings ((subject to the claims-paying ability of the insurance company). Your interest rate will be reset periodically, based on economic and other factors, but is guaranteed to never fall below a certain rate.

**FREE WITHDRAWALS** – Withdrawals that are free of surrender charges.

**INDEX** – The underlying external benchmark upon which the crediting of excess interest is based, also a measure of the prices of a group of securities.

**IRA** *(INDIVIDUAL RETIREMENT ACCOUNT)* – An IRA is a tax-advantaged personal savings plan that lets an individual set aside money for retirement. All or part of the participant's contributions may be tax deductible, depending on the type of IRA chosen and the participant's personal financial circumstances. Distributions from many employer-sponsored retirement plans may be eligible to be rolled into an IRA to continue tax-deferred growth until the funds are needed. An annuity can be used as an IRA; that is, IRA funds can be used to purchase an annuity.

**IRA ROLLOVER** – IRA rollover is the phrase used when an individual who has a balance in an employer-sponsored retirement plan transfers that balance into an IRA. Such an exchange, when properly handled, is a tax-advantaged transaction.

**LIQUIDITY** – The ease with which an asset is convertible to cash. An asset with high liquidity provides flexibility, in that the owner can easily convert it to cash at any time, but it also tends to decrease profitability.

**MARKET RISK** – The risk of the market value of an asset fluctuating up or down over time. In a fixed or fixed indexed annuity, the original principal and credited interest are not subject to market risk. Even if the index declines, the annuity owner would receive no less than their original principal back if they decided to cash in the policy at the end of the surrender period. Unlike a security, indexed annuities guarantee the original premium and the premium is backed by, and is as safe as, the insurance company that issued it (subject to the claims-paying ability of the insurance company).

**METHODOLOGY** *(ALSO SEE CREDITING METHOD)* – The way that interest crediting is calculated. On fixed indexed annuities, there are a variety of different methods used to determine how index movement becomes interest credited.

**MINIMUM GUARANTEED RETURN** *(MINIMUM INTEREST RATE)* – Fixed indexed annuities typically provide a minimum guaranteed return over the life of the contract. At the time that the owner chooses to terminate the contract, the cash surrender value is compared to a second value calculated using the minimum guaranteed return and the higher of the two values is paid to the annuity owner.

**OPTION** – A contract which conveys to its holder the right, but not the obligation, to buy or sell something at a specified price on or before a given date. After this given date the option ceases to exist. Insurers typically buy options to provide for the excess interest potential. Options may be American style whereby they may be exercised at any time prior to the given date, or they may have to be exercised only during a specified window. Options that may only be exercised during a specified period are European-style options.

**OPTION RISK** – Most insurers create the potential for excess interest in an indexed annuity by buying options. Say that you could buy a share of stock for $50. If you bought the stock and it rose to $60 you could sell it and net a $10 profit. But, if the stock price fell to $40 you'd have a $10 loss. Instead of buying the actual stock, we could buy an option that gave us the right to buy the stock for $50 at any time over the next year. The cost of the option is $2. If the stock price rose to $60 we would exercise our option, buy the stock at $50 and make $10 (less the $2 cost of the option). If the price of the stock fell to $40, $30 or $10, we wouldn't use the option and it would expire. The loss is limited to $2—the cost of the option.

**PARTICIPATION RATE** – The percentage of positive index movement credited to the annuity. If the index methodology determined that the index increased 10 percent and the indexed annuity participated in 60 percent of the increase, it would be said that the contract has a 60 percent participation rate. Participation rates may also be expressed as asset fees or yield spreads.

**POINT-TO-POINT** – A crediting method measuring index movement from an absolute initial point to the absolute end point for a period. An index had a period starting value of 100 and a period ending value of 120. A point-to-point method would record a positive index movement of 20 [120-100] or a 20 percent positive movement [(120-100)/100]. Point-to-point usually refers to annual periods; however the phrase is also used instead of term end point to refer to multiple year periods.

**PREMIUM BONUS** – A premium bonus is additional money that is credited to the accumulation account of an annuity policy under certain conditions.

**PUT OPTION** *(ALSO SEE CALL OPTION)* – Gives the holder the right to sell an underlying security or index at a specified price on or before a given date.

**QUALIFIED ANNUITIES** *(QUALIFIED MONEY)* – Qualified annuities are annuities purchased for funding an IRA, 403(b) tax-deferred annuity or other type of retirement arrangements. An IRA or qualified retirement plan provides the tax deferral. An annuity contract should be used to fund an IRA or qualified retirement plan to benefit from an annuity's features other than tax deferral, including the safety features, lifetime income payout option and death benefit protection.

**REQUIRED MINIMUM DISTRIBUTION** *(RMD)* – The amount of money that Traditional, SEP and SIMPLE IRA owners and qualified plan participants must begin distributing from their retirement accounts by April 1 following the year they reach age 70.5. RMD amounts must then be distributed each subsequent year.

**RETURN FLOOR** – Another way of saying minimum guaranteed return.

**ROTH IRA** – Like other IRA accounts, the Roth IRA is simply a holding account that manages your stocks, bonds, annuities, mutual funds and CD's. However, future withdrawals (including earnings and interest) are typically tax-advantaged once the account has been open for five years and the account holder is age 59.5.

**RULE OF 72** – Tells you approximately how many years it takes a sum to double at a given rate. It's handy to be able to figure out, without using a calculator, that when you're earning a 6 percent return, for example, by dividing 6 percent into 72, you'll find that it takes 12 years for money to double. Conversely, if you know it took a sum twelve years to double you could divide 12 into 72 to determine the annual return (6 percent).

**SIMPLE INTEREST** *(ALSO SEE <u>COMPOUND INTEREST)</u>* – Interest is only earned on the principal balance.

**SPLIT ANNUITY** – A split annuity is the term given to an effective strategy that utilizes two or more different annuity products—one designed to generate monthly income and the other to restore the original starting principal over a set period of time.

**STANDARD & POOR'S 500** *(S&P 500)* – The most widely used external index by fixed indexed annuities. Its objective is to be a benchmark to measure and report overall U.S. stock market performance. It includes a representative sample of 500 common stocks from companies trading on the New York Stock Exchange, American Stock Exchange, and NASDAQ National Market System. The index represents the price or market value of the underlying stocks and does not include the value of reinvested dividends of the underlying stocks.

**STOCK MARKET INDEX** – A report created from a type of statistical measurement that shows up or down changes in a specific financial market, usually expressed as points and as a percentage, in a number of related markets, or in an economy as a whole (i.e. S&P 500 or New York Stock Exchange).

**SURRENDER CHARGE** – A charge imposed for withdrawing funds or terminating an annuity contract prematurely. There is no industry standard for surrender charges, that is, each annuity product has its own unique surrender charge schedule. The charge is usually expressed as a percentage of the amount withdrawn prematurely from the contract. The percentage tends to decline over time, ultimately becoming zero.

**TRADITIONAL IRA** – See IRA (Individual Retirement Account)

**TERM END POINT** – Crediting methods measuring index movements over a greater timeframe than a year or two. The opposite of an annual reset method. Also referred to as a term point-to-point method. Say that the index value was at 100 on the first day of the period. If the calculated index value was at 150 at the end of the period the positive index movement would be 50 percent (150-100/100). The company would credit a percentage of this movement as excess interest. Index movement is calculated and interest credited at the end of the term and interim movements during the period are ignored.

**TERM HIGH POINT** (HIGH WATER MARK) – A type of term end point structure that uses the highest anniversary index level as the end point. Say that the index value was at 100 on the first day of the period, reached a value of 160 at the end of a contract year during the period, and ended the period at 150. A term high point method would use the 160 value—the highest contract anniversary point reached during the period, as the end point and the gross index gain would be 60 percent (160-100/100). The company would then apply a participation rate to the gain.

**TERM YIELD SPREAD** – A type of term end point structure which calculates the total index gain for a period, computes the annual compound rate of return deducts a yield spread from the annual rate of return and then recalculates the total index gain for the period based on the net annual rate. Say that an index increased from 100 to 200 by the end of a nine year period. This is the equivalent of an 8 percent compound annual interest rate. If the annuity had a 2 percent term yield spread this would be deducted from the annual interest rate (8 percent-2 percent) and the net rate would be credited to the contract (6 percent) for each of the nine years. Total index gain may also be computed by using the highest anniversary index level as the end point.

**VARIABLE ANNUITY** – A contract issued by an insurance company offering separate accounts invested in a wide variety of stocks and/or bonds. The investment risk is borne by the annuity owner. Variable annuities are considered securities and require appropriate securities registration.

**1035 EXCHANGE** – The 1035 exchange refers to the section of tax code that allows annuity owners the flexibility to exchange one annuity for another without incurring any immediate tax liabilities. This action is most often utilized when an annuity holder decides they want to upgrade an annuity to a more favorable one, but they do not want to activate unnecessary tax liabilities that would typically be encountered when surrendering an existing annuity contract.

**401(K) ROLLOVER** – See IRA Rollover